THE LOST SHIPS OF PISA

THE LOST SHIPS OF PISA

Michael H. Sedge

ibooks

NEW YORK
www.ibooks.net

DISTRIBUTED BY SIMON & SCHUSTER

An Original Publication of ibooks, inc.

Copyright © 2002 Michael H. Sedge

An ibooks, inc. Book

ibooks, inc.
24 West 25th Street
New York, NY 10010

The ibooks World Wide Web site Address is:
http://www.ibooks.net

ISBN 0-7434-5265-8
First ibooks, inc. printing October 2002
10 9 8 7 6 5 4 3 2 1

Edited by Kelly Smith

Cover art copyright © 2002 Michael H. Sedge
Jacket design by Eric Goodman
Interior design by Gilda Hannah

Printed in the U.S.A.

Luca, this one's for you.—M.S.

ACKNOWLEDGMENTS

I would first like to thank Angelo Bottini, Superintendent of Archae-ology for the Region of Tuscany, for allowing me access to and use of the scientific records, documentation, and graphic materials surrounding the San Rossore archaeological project.

My sincere thanks also go to the many people and organizations that assisted in making this book possible, particularly Alvisa Passigli, Anna Taylor, Dario Giugliano, Domenico Carro, Giovanni Viale, Jon Hall, Paolo Emilio Bagnoli, Rosario D'Agata, Stefano Bruni, the office of the Italian Minister of National Heritage, and the City Council of Pisa.

I am also in debt to the group of highly skilled professionals of Co.Idra. While juggling a thousand tasks, Debora Giorgi always found time to help—making this a better book than it would have otherwise been.

Finally, thanks to my editors, Dinah Dunn and Kelly Smith, for their insight and judgment.

Contents

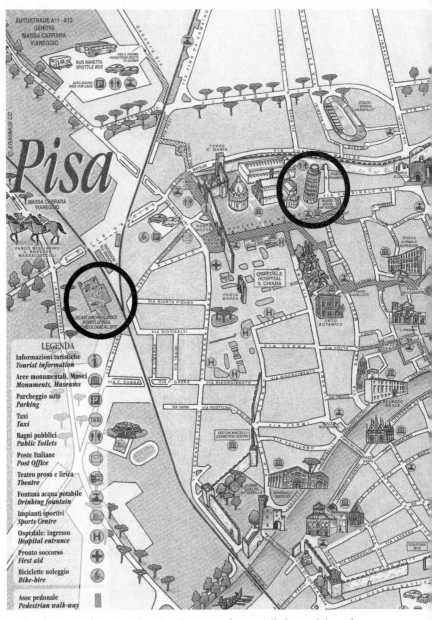

Map of Pisa indicating the San Rossore dig site (left circle) and the Leaning Tower of Pisa (right circle)

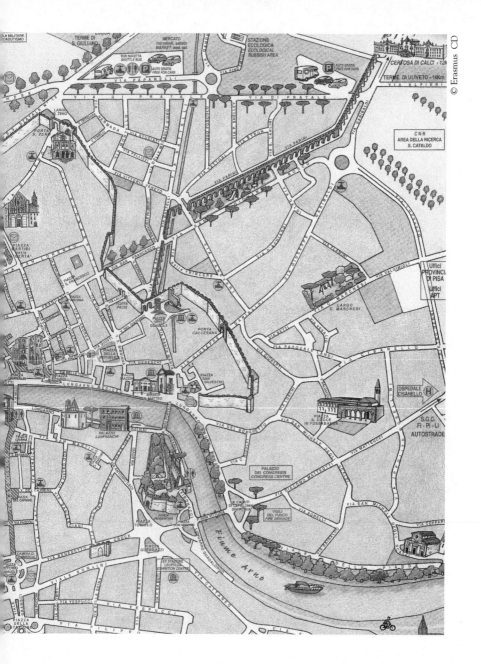

DISCLAIMER

It is my hope that *The Lost Ships of Pisa* will enlighten readers and assist researchers for decades. However, because of the nature of scientific inquiry, there will certainly be new discoveries and research in the months and years ahead. Perhaps these findings will result in inaccuracies in the current text, as well as in new theories proposed by archaeologists and scientists involved in this project.

Yet it is my promise to the reader that great effort has been made to ensure the material presented in this work is accurate at the time of this writing. Tomorrow morning I may receive a phone call informing me that another ship has been found, or a hoard of amphorae, or a mass of human bones that appear to have been those of slaves. But the facts and theories as we know them, today, appear on the following pages.

THE LOST SHIPS OF PISA

Why, When, and What If

I gazed from my office window at cotton-white clouds dancing around the crest of Mount Vesuvius, in Italy. The afternoon sun beckoned me to abandon all thoughts of completing my current writing project. For a week I had been procrastinating, putting off my current assignment. Any fleeting thoughts of delaying it yet another day vanished, fortunately, with the ringing of the telephone.

"Hello."

"Mike, how are you? This is John Buffalo."

In 1994, when we first met, John Buffalo was a U.S. Navy lieutenant aboard the USS *Belknap* in Gaeta, Italy. Since then, he had transitioned his military career into a job with the Discovery Channel in Bethesda, Maryland.

"John," I said. "A pleasant surprise. Anything exciting happening on your side of the world?"

"No. But it is on yours," he answered. "Have you heard about Pisa?"

"What about it? Is the tower falling?"

Following a forced chuckle, he continued, "It appears that a couple of ancient Roman ships have been found. In good condition from what I hear."

Having been in Pisa several times and knowing the nearby coastal areas, I asked, "Were they found in Marina di Pisa?"

"That's probably the most interesting aspect of all," John said. "According to the report I received, they found them about 15 meters underground and only 500 meters from the Leaning Tower. If true, I think it would be a great story for your archaeology magazine. Our Discovery Online editor might also have some interest in coverage."

One of the requisites of any good journalist is an insatiable curiosity. One must possess a natural thirst for knowledge and never tire of asking those childlike questions that often cause frustration among parents and teachers. Questions like why, when, and what if.

It is this form of curiosity that has stimulated me to write for nearly a quarter of a century. There seems to have been an endless array of circumstances that triggered within me the "what if" question, taking me from one project to the next.

Having spent most of my adult life in southern Italy certainly contributed to my inquisitive nature, particularly in the field of archaeology. Its streets have felt the footsteps of Julius Caesar, Cleopatra, St. Peter, and Charlemagne. It is a maze of history and seductive charm that beckons like the mythological Siren. After reporting for clients such as *Newsweek,* Time Life, and Mobil Oil's *Compass Magazine,* I became part of a Discovery Channel team working with French archaeologist, Franck Goddio, in Alexandria, Egypt. Our efforts would ultimately result in the Discovery Channel book and TV documentary, "Cleopatra's Palace: In Search of a Legend."

About this same time, archaeologist and publisher Jeff Leach was selecting staff for a new *Scientific American* magazine called *Discovering Archaeology*. I began working with the magazine as a result of my recent experience in Egypt and soon found myself traveling throughout southern Europe, the Middle East, and North Africa, like Indiana Jones in search of ancient worlds. From the 5,000-year-old temple of Hagar Qim in Malta and the ruins of Yodefat in Israel to the rebirth of wines in ancient Pompeii, the Roman city consumed by volcanic ash from Mount Vesuvius in 79 AD, and the discovery of 50,000-year-old Neanderthals in Spain, I began covering the Mediterranean region. In each instance I sought to answer the questions why, when, how, and what if.

"When I read about the ships," continued John Buffalo, "I knew it would be something you'd want to cover."

He was right.

Fifteen minutes later I was on the phone to Cecilia Mastrantonio, director of press relations at the Italian

Ministry for National Heritage. She confirmed the find and informed me that there would be a press conference the following month. So, on the cold, wet morning of April 20, 1999, I found my way to San Rossore, the excavation site near the heart of Pisa.

"It's a graveyard of ancient ships," one journalist whispered as we made our way down the steps and into the excavation area below. Beneath the protection of metal canopies, the wooden remnants of four ancient ships came into view.

"What you see," explained Debora Giorgi, one of 12 archaeologists working on the project, "are just some of the ships that were first discovered. One can only guess how many more have yet to be excavated in the surrounding area."

The dramatic discovery of what Italian authorities were calling "the Pompeii of maritime archaeology" began in December 1998 in San Rossore, when the national railroad, Ferrovie dello Stato, began digging the foundation for a new building that would house the command and control center for train movements along Italy's western coast. Upon initial digging, however, the work abruptly stopped when, to the astonishment of all, the haunting remains of a wooden, Roman ship came to light after being buried for more than 2,000 years.

"These are not the first Roman ships recovered in land excavations," explained Stefano Bruni, scientific director of the Pisa-San Rossore project. "This site is unique, however, in the number of ships recovered—at this point, 10, dating from the third century BC to the fifth century AD—and the exceptional state of preservation."

The original timbers used in the sideboards, the planking, and the beams of the ships were fully intact in most cases. This, Bruni said, was because the terrain in which the vessels were found was damp and contained relatively no oxygen, an essential element for the decay process.

During the initial excavation of the site, which measures approximately 100 by 45 meters, ships were labeled with alphabetical identification. As I looked upon the excavation site, ships labeled A through G were in various phases of recovery. The largest of these, though not yet fully visible, was ship A. Found in the northeast corner of the site, it was estimated the vessel was 30 meters in length. Unlike the other ships, the cargo of this craft was not present. The fact that the ship was found on its side, at a northern inclination, might be a clue to the lack of cargo. Items it carried could have easily spilled into the sea when the vessel sank.

Along the eastern edge of the site was ship B, a craft believed to have been used for transporting cargo. The 10-

meter ship, constructed of a double layer of wood, fixed with bronze spikes, contained a cargo of amphorae, the giant vase-like containers used by the ancient Greeks and Romans to hold wine, fruit juices, olives, and other food stuffs. Scientific analysis of residue would reveal the containers once held the juices of fruit such as peaches and cherries, as well as chestnuts; there would also be traces of olives and sand. Further analysis would reveal that the sand originated from Campania, a region of southern Italy. Bricks, rocks, fragments of marble, and lava blocks, along with bronze coins imprinted with Roman Emperor Agrippa, cups, plates, and a variety of other items, were found in the bowels of the ship.

While each ship, apart from A, had similar contents, and were more or less in upright positions, vessel D, which experts initially believed to be a warship, was found upside down in the center of the excavation site. This presented an interesting challenge to the archaeological team.

"This 14-meter-long, 6-meter-wide craft contains a structure unlike any other Roman vessel found to date," according to the reports of researchers. "The external sideboards are reinforced with rough, wooden poles, running parallel along the length of the craft, beginning at the bow."

Experts from the Center of Restoration of the Super-intendent of Archaeology for the Region of Tuscany, I learned, were working simultaneously with archaeologists to maintain the humidity of the wooden structures, while applying protective layers of varnish to avoid decay, prior to final excavation and transportation to a nearby warehouse-laboratory.

Besides the ancient seagoing vessels, archaeologists at the San Rossore site had recovered more than 400 amphorae and other artifacts of Punic—stemming from the ancient peoples of Carthage, on the coast of northern Africa—and Roman style, dating from the second century AD. While many of these were part of the ships' cargo, others were found dispersed throughout the excavation site in what one archaeologist called a "river of antiquities."

"In addition to the array of amphorae, we've found hobnails, coins, ceramic vases, tiny bottles; and I have seen a beautiful lamp in *terra sigillati*, the red pottery of the first century BC," explained Paolo Emilio Bagnoli of the Department of Information Engineering, University of Pisa, and member of the Gruppo Archaeologicao Pisano. "With ship C there were also objects of daily use, such as a bag for clothing, a sandal, and a twisted rope. There was also a large amount of stone choppers that were the ballast of the ships. Many of these came from the Island of Elba. There were also pieces of firestone from Mount Vesuvius." A tiny gold pin and other personal effects had also emerged as daily excavations continued.

Apart from the recoveries, according to Stefano Bruni, the discovery of this port of antiquity was a major find in itself.

"This is a complete mystery," he pointed out. "Until now, there was no contemporary knowledge of a commercial port in Pisa. We are, therefore, trying to put together a picture of the city's ancient topography, in addition to our archaeological work."

Careful excavation along the southeastern edge of the site—where future digging was planned—had also brought to light the nearly intact remains of the ancient pier structure.

Prior to the finds at San Rossore, historians believed the area to have been a backwater, stemming from two parallel rivers, the Arno, which continues to flow through Pisa, and the Auser, which dried up centuries ago. Based on the methodical excavations and discoveries of Professor Bruni's team, experts now believe that a complex system of lagoons linked to the sea—currently 4 kilometers from the site—had been established by the Romans. Along this waterway the urban port of ancient Pisa, estimated to have been in operation between the fifth century BC and fifth century AD, was constructed.

"This find lets us, above all else, look at the physiognomy of the ancient passages to the city of Pisa in a new light, and explore its port, which, until now, was completely unknown," explained Bruni.

But what happened more than 2 millennia ago to cause the entombing of an entire port? That was my thought as I left the press conference and headed toward Galileo Galilei International Airport for a flight back to Naples. While many were asking the same question, few, at this point, were speculating.

"You must remember," one researcher said, "that until now we did not know that an ancient port ever existed in this area of Pisa. All of this has taken place in less than 120 days."

While experts did not know the exact history of the Roman ships of Pisa, their future was certain. According to the Superintendent of Archaeology for the Region of Tuscany, Angelo Bottini, the ships, once fully excavated, would be taken to the nearby Arsenali Mediciei. This structure, used in the sixteenth century for shipbuilding and storage along the River Arno, would be transformed into a temporary laboratory-museum for the subsequent phase of restoration and an ultimate "Ships of Pisa" exhibit.

"It could take 1½ to 2 years for this next phase. During

this time the ships will be immersed in tanks of water," said Bottini. "Thereafter, in the subsequent stages of restoration, we may be able to allow viewing by the public. We are talking a minimum of three years, however."

Sitting next to me aboard the Alitalia flight to Rome was Giovanna Melandri, minister of National Heritage. Her presence at the press conference confirmed the Italian State's dedication to ensuring the excavations continued. She would eventually request government funding, in addition to that already obligated for the project, to cover further research, restoration, and construction of a permanent museum for the ships of Pisa.

"The importance of this excavation is immediately obvious," Melandri told reporters. "We have the base here for an exceptional museum of ancient naval vessels. It is truly a maritime Pompeii."

In the days that followed the press conference, as I worked on an article for the July 1999 issue of *Scientific American Discovering Archaeology*, my subconscious haunted me with questions that stimulated my journalistic curiosity. What would the archaeological puzzle reveal? What devastating event occurred in history to create the graveyard of ships that was being unveiled in Pisa? And what of the ancient port? How had such an important aspect of the city escaped historians? Would these and other questions be answered as researchers put the pieces of the puzzle together?

I wondered.

The only way for me to know, and to satisfy my inquisitiveness, would be to follow the research and excavations as they developed. Over the next two years, as the slices of ancient life came to light, the finds would reveal far more than was initially believed possible. Hundreds of thousands of artifacts beyond the ships, including human and animal remains, emerged, as did theories on what had taken place during the ancient port's last 1,000 years.

As time passed, my archive of documentation grew. Each week new discoveries were being made and new research was being revealed. It was also evident that what had started with a phone call from a friend had now become a major passion in my life.

This realization germinated the idea of writing a book on Pisa's ships, to share my passion with archaeology enthusiasts throughout the world.

This book is the result of my investigations and efforts to fit together the pieces of the archaeological puzzle. This book is not a definitive work; it cannot be, for the excavations and search for the truth behind the lost ships of Pisa is a work-in-progress. Just last week, one researcher expressed that the archaeological digging could go on for another 20 years or more. In the meantime, join me in this quest to reveal the mysteries of the lost ships of Pisa and answer the questions why, when, and what if.

Opposite: An ancient incense burner

A CITY BY THE SEA

The young, aristocratic woman rose to her feet as the ship in which she traveled was navigated through the backwaters of the River Auser and into the Porto della Conche, the port of this Roman Empire city. At last they had arrived in Pisa, the city named after one of its mythical founders, Piseus. Struggling to maintain her balance, the clasp fastening her outer garment—made of gold, symbolizing her social status, rather than those traditionally gilded in bronze, iron, and silver—snapped, one piece catching on the rough fabric, the other lodging between the rugged floorboards of the 10-meter, wooden marine vessel. Here it would lie, unseen, for over 2 millennia.

The 27-year-old paleontologist from the University of Pisa, cut through the mud along the outer edge of the decayed Roman ship with an archaeologist's trowel. It was only 10 a.m., but she had already asked herself a dozen times what she was doing here. Sure, it was an emergency situation and the Superintendent of Archaeology had called upon every specialist in the Tuscan region, but she much preferred scavenging ancient caverns for the remains of prehistoric reptiles.

Over the past four months several Roman ships had been uncovered within the construction area of what was to be the national railway's new San Rossore Command and Control Center building, a short distance from Pisa's historical center. The Superintendent of Archaeology had been given full access and cooperation to the area by the state railway, Ferrovie dello Stato, with one stipulation: there was a time limit requiring that artifacts be removed as quickly as possible to allow for the continued construction of the new building. All available archaeologists and researchers in Pisa, Florence, and surrounding areas, including students and volunteers from such organizations as the Gruppo Archaeologicao Pisano, were therefore called upon to assist in this massive task.

Initially the paleontologist had been thrilled. After all, they had already uncovered thousands of artifacts—amphorae, oil lamps, statuary, coins—in addition to the ships. But now the tedious, unglamorous work that all archaeologists experience was beginning to set in. Today she had been assigned to ship C, which, much like the famed tower only 500 meters away, inclined at a 45-degree angle in the center of the 3-acre excavation site.

The previous night's rain had caused thick, dark mud to form in the terrain surrounding the aged vessel, making her job miserable. She maneuvered the trowel to and fro in the moistened earth. To and fro, to and fro, to and . . .

Click.

. . . fro.

"What was that," she whispered, retracing the path of the masonry tool.

Click.

It was a light sound, hardly a noise at all. More a feeling, like that a fisherman senses when a fish is nibbling at the bait.

Slowly she eased her fingers outward and into the cold, soft mud, wrapping them around a tiny object.

She then eagerly dipped her hand into her nearby washing bucket, moving it round and round and round before pulling it out. Between her fingers the gold object—long, pointed, and coiled at one end—glistened in the soft morning sun. The paleontologist had not noticed the increase in her heartbeat as she raised the piece for closer examination.

"A pin," she whispered. "Or part of a pin."

The find would eventually be identified as a fibula, a clasp or pin used in ancient Greece and Rome for fastening garments. Like all objects at the site, it would be registered by location and description for additional study. In this case, the official log would read:

Pisa San Rossore 2 South extension Sector 1, Layer 50,

Artificial layer II. A small part of the end of the (fibula) bow, the spring and the pin are preserved. The bow
has a flattened cross section with a longitudinal rib
defined by lateral grooves; the end is rounded with two
small pointed lateral winglets. The spring has four
coils, which are symmetrical with respect to the pin;
the connecting wire is internal and covered by the
bow. The straight pin seems to have preserved its original length, judging from the pointed tip.

A smile eased from the corner of the young paleontologist's mouth, then illuminated her face. "What stories do you
have to tell?" she asked, bringing the fibula closer.

"Much of Pisa's history is bound up with the sea," explained Gino Nunes, president of the province of Pisa. "The
discoveries made at the excavation site . . . will make it possible to reconstruct a historical, cultural, and environmental
picture of this city of great interest and appeal for both habit-
ual and occasional visitors."

Despite the archaeological trove, it is impossible to reconstruct the ancient maritime landscape of Pisa based on these
finds alone. Each of the ships, each of the relics, needs to be
placed into a historical content. For this we need to review
the centuries of development that have led to contemporary

Pisa, the Italian city that entices millions of visitors a year with its famed Leaning Tower.

The masterpieces that rise up from the lavish, green grasses of Piazza del Duomo—the area in which the city's cathedral and Leaning Tower are located—bear witness to the greatness of the maritime republic that was Pisa in the Middle Ages. Similarly, the nearby Arsenals of the Cittadella are visible illustrations of the important role this city played in maintaining the maritime policy of the Grand Duchy of the Medici family. But the city's history and tradition with the sea extend back further in time.

The ancient Roman naturalist and author, Pliny (23–79 AD), mentioned Piseus, the legendary founder of Pisa, in his *Natural History*, attributing him with the invention of the rostrum, the beaklike projection at the bow of warships used for ramming enemy vessels. Earlier yet, Strabo (circa 63 BC–19 AD), the Greek geographer, referenced the ancient city and its docks linked to the sea.

Archaeological finds, including those of San Rossore, west of the city's medieval walls and walking distance from Piazza del Duomo, testify to a human presence in Pisa during the Eneolithic age, in the third millennium BC. There is also evidence of settlements by the Etruscans, the highly civilized population that reached its zenith in the modern-day region of Tuscany around 500 BC. Subsequently, as the Romans took control of the entire Italian peninsula, Pisa fell under their dominance.

The earliest colonists along the northwestern coast of Italy, known as Liguria, were probably of Celtic origin. They anticipated Greek colonization here by a few thousand years. Just the same, most likely there was a transition period where the Celtic and Greek peoples traded and exchanged cultural habits.

"Even though the legend of Pelops—who supposedly left the shores of the River Alfeo, in Peloponnesus, the southern peninsula of Greece, for those of the River Arno to found Pisa, in perennial memory of his land of origin—is indirectly supported by Virgil, the Roman poet, in the tenth book of the *Aeneid*, we know with certainty that Pisa was an early port of call in trading with the Greeks," says one expert, on the city's official website, PisaOnLine.

During the time of the Etruscans, the village of Pisa developed around a complex lagoon system, linking the city to the Mediterranean coast. It was a region marked by two rivers, the Arno and the Auser. Today, the Auser has completely disappeared. There were also numerous minor waterways, giving Pisa an atmosphere similar to modern-day Venice.

Inasmuch as the ancient village was susceptible to coastal instability and periodical floods, its relationship to the sea provided the resources for it to develop as a great fishing and shipbuilding center. From its geographical position on the border of Etruria, in west-central Italy, Pisa joined forces with Rome in the wars against the Ligurians, who populated northwest territories of the peninsula, and the Carthaginians, who came from the coast of northern Africa.

Early Greek and Roman literary references are made to the Port of Pisa—Portus Pisanus—which was said to be located at the mouth of a river where the contemporary basilica of San Piero a Grando now stands. It was here, according to legend, that the apostle Peter docked, spending a short time in Pisa prior to making his final journey to Rome.

Using the Port of Pisa, the Roman fleet was able to wage attacks on the Ligurians and the Gauls, from northern Europe, as well as orchestrate naval maneuvers along the coasts of Corsica, Sardinia, and Spain.

By the time Roman Emperor Octavian Augustus took power in the first century BC, Pisa had become an official Roman colony, taking the name Colonia Julia Pisanan Obsequens (Julia Pisanan, colony willing to serve and obey). The city experienced a period of rapid growth in commerce and shipbuilding, as well as population and territorial expansion, as Roman roadways like Via Aurelia and Via Aemilia Scaurii linked it to the mainland. During this time the first protective walls were also constructed around Pisa.

In addition to the mighty rivers and military port that supported the Roman naval and commercial maritime activities of ancient Pisa, historians make reference to an urban harbor and corresponding wet docks, which, thanks to the recent finds at San Rossore, we now know were situated west of the city's center in the Middle Ages.

"At the moment there are no elements to collocate chronologically when this port, situated inside a settlement area that dates back at least to the end of the ninth century BC, began to be used," said Stefano Bruni, technical and scientific director of the San Rossore project. "On the contrary, much material, which probably fell in the water during unloading, makes it possible to fix when the port stopped being used—or at least this part of it—during the latter part of the fifth century or at the beginning of the sixth century AD, significantly in coincidence with the collapse of the Roman urban system."

Bruni went on to say, in a report for the Italian, daily newspaper, *La Repubblica*, that, "Not by chance in the more surface levels relative to the life of this harbor substantial remains of mosaic pavements, frescoed walls, stuccos, and marble structures have been retrieved, as well as a small marble statue bearing evident traces of its ancient restoration, the abandoning of which in the port area is probably connected with the demolition of certain city buildings in the imperial age."

Apart from the Baths of Hadrian—incorrectly called the Baths of Nero—there remains little of the grandiose private and public construction that took place during Pisa's imperial era. This, according to experts, is due to subsequent demolitions and rebuilding of the city. Archaeological research, however, provides evidence that numerous temples—most replaced by churches at the rise of Christianity—a Forum, Palatium, Amphitheatre, and Naval Circus once adorned the city landscape.

The apostle Peter has been attributed with bringing Christianity to Pisa in 47 AD. Upon this legend, which may or may not hold some grain of truth, the people subsequently constructed a basilica on the site where the saint had supposedly made landfall.

The Lombards, then the Franks, took control of the city following the fall of the Roman Empire. In the Middle Ages, as one historian put it, "the city's maritime vocation burgeoned and soon contrasted with the Saracens, who were aiming for full supremacy of the Mediterranean. With bases in Corsica and Sardinia, the Saracens frequently threatened the lands controlled by the Church."

Following several years of attacks, the Pisans, from 1016 to 1052, began to conquer the Tyrrhenian Sea and the lands within it. Sardinia and Corsica came under their control, and soon, with papal consent, the Pisan fleet sailed to Sicily where they joined Norman Roger I against the Saracens.

One record of the attacks tells that, "After breaking the chains of the harbor of Palermo, the ships hoisting the Pisan Cross in a field of red, defeated the enemy, returning home in 1062 with such rich booty that they were able to begin construction of a new cathedral."

Nine hundred thirty-nine years after Pisa's victory over the Saracens, the great cathedral still stands. Built upon the ruins of what was, in the first century, the Palatium of Emperor Hadrian, and subsequently the church of Santa Reparata, the white marble masterpiece appeared, during much of the first millennium, almost surreal in contrast with the blue sky and encompassing emerald turf. Its construction, financed with the spoils of war, had been tasked to Buscheto di Giovanni Giudice in 1063, whose architectural goal was to glorify both God and the magnificents of the maritime republic of Pisa.

Pope Gelasius II had dedicated the structure, designed in

a Latin cross with five naves and three transepts, in 1118. It was not until the turn of the century, however, that architect and native Pisan, Rainaldo, completed the façade.

Separate from the array of arches and columns, the medieval, tufa-stone wall frames the piazza's north and west sides. Now knowing that the recently found Roman ships were less than 500 meters away, it was easy to imagine Pisa in ancient times, when these walls, streets, and edifices embraced an urban harbor where ships loaded with cargoes from Mediterranean ports were docked, ready for loading and offloading.

The Pisan fleet played a major role in the first crusade, which also allowed the maritime republic to extend its commercial activities into Near Eastern ports, in particular Constantinople. Over the next 200 years, the city-state would conquer the Balearic Isles, defeat Amalfi, and become a supreme maritime and military power in the Mediterranean Sea. Its commercial status equaled that of its rich sister port, Venice, during this period. The glory of Pisa would not last long, however.

During this period, Genoa, a sea power in its own right, launched numerous maritime battles against Pisa, its long-time rival. Its efforts dramatically damaged not only the Pisan military, but its commerce throughout the Mediterranean. Simultaneously, the city came under land attacks from the Guelph cities of Tuscany, which supported the authority of the Pope, as opposed to aristocratic rule. By 1300, the combination of sea and land assaults had destroyed Pisa's power.

Over the next 100 years, the maritime city would become a chip in high-stakes trading, being handed to the lords of Milan in 1392, then sold to the Florentines in 1405. The once-glorious maritime republic next fell under the rule of French King Charles VIII, but in 1509, returned once again to the powers in Florence.

One might say that the salvation of Pisa came at the hands of the Medici government of Cosimo I. The Medici family ruled Florence and, later, Tuscany from the fifteenth to the eighteenth centuries. Members of this noble family included three popes and royalty, by marriage, throughout Europe. Their fortune came in banking, and historians have attributed much of Italy's Renaissance splendor to their support of the arts. It was, in fact, the Medici family that supported such masters as Brunelleschi, Donatello, Fra Angelico, Leonardo da Vinci, and Michelangelo.

A descendent of Lorenzo de' Medici, known throughout history as Lorenzo the Magnificent, Cosimo I was proclaimed grand duke of Tuscany by Pope Pius V in 1569. This would trigger a period of renaissance for the city of Pisa, with university activities on the rise and a variety of public and private construction projects. This was also the time in which the Order of the Knights of St. Stephen originated. Pisa had always maintained its status as a seaport, although very small in comparison to what it had once been. Under the Order of the Knights, in the sixteenth century, however, there was a revival of the city's ancient maritime traditions.

But it was the maritime policy of the Grand Duchy of the Medici family that returned the city to its full glory. Medici rulers following Cosimo I were responsible for such public works as the Aqueduct of Asciano in 1601 and, 2 years later, the Canal of the Navicelli, which ran from Pisa to Livorno. Another Middle Ages' contribution to the maritime industry was the Medici Arsenals, located along the shores of the Arno, where shipbuilding reached its zenith.

During the Renaissance, the series of large, arched rooms that make up the Medici Arsenals were alive with shipbuilding activity, with orders coming in from all parts of the Italian peninsula. As centuries passed, however, more and more business passed to Genoa and the shipbuilding ports of other Mediterranean nations, leaving the once-thriving Medici Arsenals abandoned and decayed. But in 1999, the ironic twist of fate created by the archaeological discoveries at San Rossore, resurrected the arsenals, this time to house the ancient Roman ships and their cargoes. One of the excavation directors explained:

> The discovery of the Roman ships of San Rossore has posed numerous problems of various types from the beginning. First and foremost, the choice of methodology of field research . . . resolution of these problems immediately placed another important matter in the foreground: that of a museum. Where can such spacious areas be found that would allow for adequate housing not only for the finds, but also for all of the scientific and educational materials that a discovery of this kind generates?
>
> The identification of a museum space in the Medici Arsenals has solved the problem in the best possible way. There, where Pisa had developed its naval power, it will be possible to concretely re-create the history of Roman Pisa's relationship with the river and with the sea.

In anticipation of the recovery of the ancient vessels, in 1999, funding had already been allocated and the Medici Arsenals were currently under renovation. The discoveries of San Rossore were taking a high priority on the agenda of local, regional, and national politicians, and rightly so. For as one researcher put it:

> We must not forget that the ships and their cargoes, according to the politics of museum decentralization, successfully put into practice by the Ministry for Cultural Heritage in recent years, will not be moved by much compared to where they were buried for 2,000 years, thus enriching the city's heritage, which, from now on, will be given worldwide recognition not only as the city of the Leaning Tower, but also as that of the Roman ships.

Various theories, based on the new finds, hypothesized that the River Arno, combined with the now nonexistent Auser, had formed the base for a series of canals and backwaters that supported the city's historical port.

A report from the Cooperativa Indagine Documentazione Ricerca Archaelogica (Co.Idra), the support group responsible for the documentation and visual recording of the excavations of San Rossore stated:

> On one hand, the discovery allows the problem of the

location of the city-port of Pisa to be defined in more certain and objective terms, which is not a minor issue in the reconstruction of Pisa's historical events . . . . On the other hand, the discovery is turning out to be of extreme interest for the reconstruction of life in this great ancient city port and its maritime traffic in the Mediterranean between the latter decade of the fifth century BC until the fifth century of the Christian era.

A breakwater palisade has been identified in the San Rossore area, discovered still in place, and a pier, which had collapsed centuries ago, made of large, stone blocks. This supported an adjacent construction, built of smaller stones, from which another palisade projected. About 10 meters to the north was a smaller, wooden pier, partly destroyed at the time of its discovery.

The San Rossore excavations, when properly inserted in the historical context of Pisa, would shed light on the city's past as well as that of ancient maritime activities in the Mediterranean. These excavations would also give rise to very important questions: How could a city harbor of such importance in Etruscan and Roman times go forgotten to modern history? At what point did the port become so obsolete that records ceased to mention it? And what events were responsible for creating the graveyard of ships that were now coming to light in the San Rossore area of the city? The answer to these and other questions—in fact, the answer to this maritime mystery—may still lie among the archaeological discoveries that have emerged after hiding beneath the centuries'-old layers of soil that ultimately engulfed the port of ancient Pisa.

If anyone was capable of answering these questions, it was Professor Stefano Bruni.

Opposite: The San Rossore excavation site, during the early phases of development, called for extensive engineering not only to ensure the safety of the ships, but to maintain the humidity levels and avoid flooding from seeping waters.

CHAPTER TWO

A PORT
IS FOUND

While Italy is traditionally a slow, bureaucratic country when it comes to financial, logistical, and government support of scientific projects, in the 5 months following the discovery of the first Roman ship, the "emergency" archaeological team put together by Stefano Bruni, technical and scientific director of the San Rossore project, and Angelo Bottini, Superintendent of Archaeology for the Region of Tuscany, with the cooperation and backing of Giovanna Melandri, minister of National Heritage, had astonished the world. Ten well-preserved Roman ships had been partially or fully unearthed. It was the largest group of ancient vessels to be found in a single area. The ships were nearly intact, including the copper nails that held them together.

In addition, cargoes still remained in some holds, while more lay spread across the floor of the massive pit that had been slowly and carefully excavated. A temporary concrete floor had been laid around the vessels and the countless amphorae, oil lamps, pottery, and other artifacts that surrounded the ships. It was an archaeologist's dream come true. Study of the vessels would greatly add to the knowledge of Roman shipbuilding techniques, while classical trading in the Mediterranean, including that of fruit, olives, and wine, would be revealed through analysis of the cargoes.

Stefano Bruni sported a thin beard and wire-framed glasses. Clad in a scholarly looking tweed jacket, and with pipe in hand, he explained that he had initially been called in by Superintendent Bottini to survey the site in April of the previous year. After numerous core tests, he declared the soil sterile, and the Italian state railway, Ferrovia dello Stato, was given approval to begin construction. Ironically, his tests had been conducted only 3 inches short of one of the most dramatic maritime archaeological discoveries of the century.

Soon after construction began, workers came upon the first vessel, which they bisected while sinking a corrugated steel retaining wall. And despite his specialization in Etruscan history at the Istituto Nazionale di Studi Etruschi ed Italici, Bruni found himself tasked to direct the excavation project.

My first question to Professor Bruni was not unique. He had, in fact, probably answered it hundreds of times in the previous weeks, as journalists from around the world—ABC News, *Archaeology Magazine*, BBC, CNN, *Discover Magazine*, *The New York Times*—began learning of this unique, maritime treasure. Nevertheless, it was my job to ask, once again, "How could this urban port of ancient Pisa have escaped historians? Why do we have relatively little or no knowledge of it until now?"

"The environment and geographical nature of the area in which the settlement of Etruscan and Roman Pisa was born and developed is now very different from what it was in ancient times," he explained. "As a result of deposits accumulating in the Arno, the coast is now at a considerable distance, and the characteristics of the surrounding countryside have been significantly altered by the gradual expansion of marshland. This is due to the abandonment of the defenses connected with the lagoon system, the rising sea level, and the hydrological deterioration produced by the political, economical, and demographic crisis undergone by the city in late ancient times, as well as subsequent radical reclamation projects undertaken from the Middle Ages onward."

Bruni explained that there were certain historical references to an ancient harbor and waterways around Pisa, including that of Greek writer Strabo, who described a coastline, located much farther inland than that of today. He mentioned a city approximately 20 *stadia* (slightly less than 4 kilometers) from the sea and described the land between as a maze of vast lagoons flanking the massive sand bar of San Guido. With the waterways providing easy access to the sea, human settlements had developed along this sandy terrain.

In his book, *Istorie Pisane*, sixteenth-century historian

Raffaello Roncioni also talks of a harbor known as the Porto delle Conche that was formed by a secondary branch of the Auser River. In the vicinity of the Pisa dockyards, the description tells how the tributary turned right with respect to the major artery, flowing into the Arno to create a small lake.

"[The lake]," wrote Roncioni, "retains its old name and is still known today as the Porto delle Conche, at a short distance from which the small river flowed into the sea. . . ."

The historian again mentions Porto delle Conche in subsequent writings, providing its geographical location as 2 miles from Pisa. It was also mentioned that a great deal of construction materials from the Imperial Age had been recovered from this area at the beginning of the sixteenth century.

Though Roncioni is somewhat vague in his descriptions, and the topography of the region around Pisa has certainly changed over the past 500 years, Bruni believes that the referenced Porto delle Conche could easily be—and probably is—the excavation site from which the Roman ships have emerged.

"The Porto delle Conche is unanimously regarded as located in the area of the Selva del Tombolo, [a woodland on the outskirts of Pisa]," he said. "This is where the monastery of

San Rossore was founded against the backdrop of the conflict between the papacy and the Holy Roman Empire in the late eighteenth century, and its name is still used to identify the northernmost part of this area, which stretched [according to the historical writings of Roncioni] *a faucibus veteris Sircli usque ad fauces Arni* (from the throat of the old Serchio River to the mouth of the Arno). In the absence of other evidence, however, there is still a great deal of uncertainty as to the precise location of this landing place, which some remarks by Roncioni appear to describe as a full-scale harbor."

A recent reconstruction of the city's ancient hydrography confirms that a branch of the Auser split into two tributaries near the present-day soccer stadium, Arena Garibaldi. As one branch wound through the city to ultimately join the Arno, the other, as if to confirm Roncioni's history, headed north. It flowed past the medieval hospital, eventually expanding into a lakelike backwater around the area where the Pisa-San Rossore railway building was to be constructed.

Professor Bruni pointed out, "There is no evidence to identify this location as Raffaello Roncioni's Porto delle Conche, which some historians regard as a possible erudite invention of the Renaissance era. We should, however, bear in mind that in the middle of the sixteenth century, Leandro Alberti's book, *Descrittione di tutto l'Italia (Description of All*

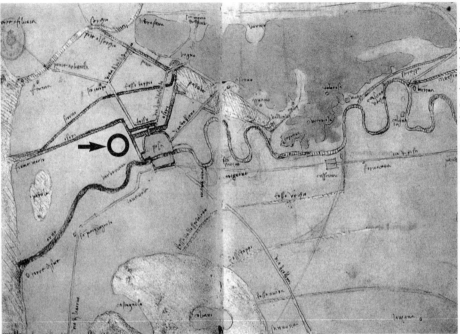

Leonardo Condice Madrid Collection

Leonardo da Vinci's map of Pisa (1503) indicating the site of the San Rossore excavations

Italy) mentions the existence of a *laghetto* or small lake between the Arno and the Serchio. This is also shown on a map of Pisa drawn by Leonardo da Vinci in 1503, and on Geronimo Bellarmato's printed map of 1536."

Andrew L. Slayman, associate editor of *Archaeology Magazine*, wrote that, "In antiquity the Porto delle Conche was evidently one of Pisa's harbors, and, as in any harbor, some

Map of Etruria by Geromino Bellarmato (1536) indicating Pisa

vessels sank or were abandoned at anchor. During the past 2,000 years, large amounts of silt washing downriver were deposited on the basin floor, covering and protecting ships as they sank and eventually filling the basin altogether."

While Slayman's description could no doubt hold true for some of the vessels, I was curious, given the overwhelming array of intact cargoes, what Bruni's theory might be regarding the fate of the ships. For it would seem that a ship left to anchor, sinking with time, would have been stripped of all valuables. Or was there another explanation for the destruction of this sunken fleet?

According to Bruni, "The boats probably sank for different reasons connected either with maneuvering errors, bad weather conditions, difficulties caused by the flooding of the river, or a combination of all of these or similar reasons."

Bruni further explained that a document in the state archives of Lucca, a city neighboring Pisa to the northeast, records a storm in 1285 in which two ships at Porto Pisano met watery fates because the sailors aboard were unable to navigate to safety through the rough waters, which ultimately engulfed them.

While some researchers consider this the answer to the destiny of some of the San Rossore ships, Professor Bruni points out that the nonrecovery of the cargoes, given the shallow depth of the seabed, does raise certain questions.

"Without too much difficulty [the limited depth] would have allowed divers to fish out the amphorae and the other items. Although there are no attestations of any kind regarding the existence of *urinatores* (deep-sea divers) in Pisa, it is very probable that, as members of a guild, frogmen must have been active in the city ports."

The real question, then, in addition to how the ships of Pisa sank, should be why importers and local traders never attempted to recover the valuable merchandise that went down with them. Non- or partial recovery of cargoes from ships submerged in ancient times, however, is not a novelty. Several recorded cases exist of ships, such as *La Madrague de Giens,* that sank during the middle of the first century BC, in which the cargo was only partially recovered.

"At the moment it is not possible to pinpoint the causes that led to the sinking of these boats," Bruni told me. "But the presence, in some cases, of part of the cargoes still in place would seem to exclude that this sector of the port once represented a kind of graveyard for old ships as, for example, has been suggested for the port of Claudius at Fiumicino (the ancient Port of Rome), which is somewhat similar to that of Pisa."

Speculation. Theories. These are all part of the archaeologist's job, and a major part of the work at San Rossore. As the pieces come together, more and more of these ideas and concepts will become concrete, or be abandoned based on the evidence revealed.

Excavations have continued, revealing an additional 6 ships—either intact or in part—bringing the total to 16. Surrounding some of the new vessels—primarily those tagged as "cargo ships"—have come additional artifacts: coins, clothing, shoes, pottery, amphorae, and bones of animals that were transported from as far off as northern Africa. The first intact human remains were also uncovered just before the turn of the new millennium—a full male skeleton. This ghost from the sea, holding the skeleton of a small dog, presents fascinating new evidence to speculate upon the victim's final moments.

The lost ships of Pisa are an archaeological work-in-progress; a search for the pieces of a puzzle that, when completed, may reveal the true story of the Porto delle Conche.

After gathering the historical background and theories surrounding this ancient port, the investigation now turned to the details of the Roman ships, for each possessed information and knowledge that promised to shed additional light on the San Rossore excavation.

Opposite: The Romans sailed the
Mediterranean Sea as if it were a lake.
In fact, they called it *Mare Nostrum*
(Our Sea).

CHAPTER THREE

THE SHIPS

Michael Sedge

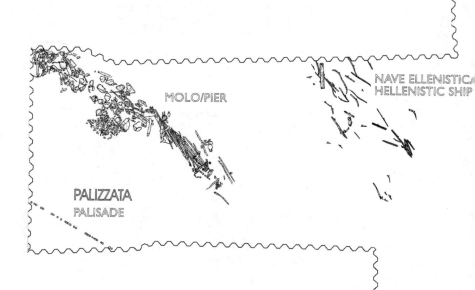

NAVE ELLENISTICA
HELLENISTIC SHIP

MOLO/PIER

PALIZZATA
PALISADE

The San Rossore excavation site

0 1 2

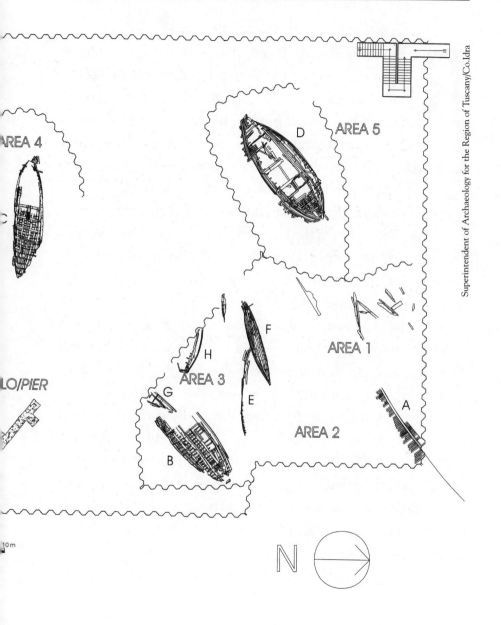

AREA 4

C

D

AREA 5

LO/PIER

AREA 1

H

F

AREA 3

G

E

B

A

AREA 2

10 m

N

Superintendent of Archaeology for the Region of Tuscany/Co.Idra

Reality and what is *perceived* as reality can often be complete opposites. A good example of this is the science of archaeology. Too much of the general public imagines that the life of an archaeologist is filled with adventure and mystery. Nothing is further from the truth. Credit for this misconception, for the most part, can be attributed to film director George Lucas and his creation of heroic archaeologist Indiana Jones. Hollywood productions like *Raiders of the Lost Ark*, *The Temple of Doom*, and *The Last Crusade*, while boosting the visibility and interest in the study of ancient life and culture, have provided an illusion that is far from reality.

Systematic archaeology is a time-consuming, painstaking process, calling for detailed record keeping. Each object and its physical condition must be recorded and studied. Frequently, the documentation process also includes detailed line drawings and photographs, followed by cataloguing and laboratory studies. All of this follows the rigid digging process that, in cases like the ships of Pisa, includes the use of contemporary preservation techniques to decrease rapid deterioration as artifacts come into contact with atmospheric conditions after centuries of protection below the surface of the earth.

Field conditions run the gamut from icy rain, creating

mud, which pulls at researchers' boots as they walk through the excavation site, to smoldering, summer sun, which leaves arms and any other unprotected areas red and blistered. These are the realities of archaeology, and the grievances faced each day by the team of professionals working the San Rossore site.

As my investigation into the Pisa project increased, so too did my respect for the researchers, particularly those working in the field. Despite popular misconceptions, their jobs were far from adventurous. I watched as, each evening, they emerged from the giant excavation pit with frozen fingers and aching backs, or sunburnt faces and worn knees. For them, finding a tiny oil lamp, a Roman coin, or a seemingly meaningless brass nail provided the excitement of a lost ark.

They are true archaeologists. They are professionals. They understand that within the most insignificant relic could lay the key that unlocks a new chapter in the constantly growing science of archaeology.

It was this spirit that drove Superintendent of Archaeology, Angelo Bottini, to the Florence-based research and documentation company, Co.Idra, when he needed professional support for the San Rossore project. Begun in 1983 in Tuscany's culture capital, Florence, Co.Idra is an organization of graduates of archaeology, architecture, geology, geography, and other sciences. Because of the expertise it offers in a wide range of academic fields, the company is frequently called upon by organizations within Italy's cultural affairs departments. Once involved, Co.Idra becomes the documentation and disclosure center for an archaeological project; and, through interdisciplinary study, a site such as San Rossore can literally come back to life.

"We're responsible for total coordination of documentation, research, charts, drawings, images, territorial studies, planning, didactic activities, animated recreations through software and computer technology, as well as artistic methods—and, in our spare time," joked Debora Giorgi, Co.Idra excavation director, "we handle exhibits and press inquiries like yours."

It was Stefano Bruni who first suggested I contact Co.Idra with my journalistic requests, as the company had established the documentation headquarters for the San Rossore excavations. My goal during this visit was to obtain a general overview and scientific data regarding the recovered ships to date.

Upon entering the office spaces, however, I encountered a researcher's paradise; it was as if I had stepped onto the set of an Indiana Jones film. Walls were covered in charts, maps, and drawings. One room contained catalogued images, in trays, in boxes, and on viewing tables. Text reports had been condensed onto floppy discs and CDs, including a complete archive of the field research, the scientific reports, and the printed documentation. At one computer, technicians were working on an animated reconstruction of the Porto delle Conche—which most experts believe to be the site currently excavated—and how it might have appeared in ancient times. This would ultimately become part of a video presentation for The Ancient Ships of San Rossore Museum.

"The first ship was found in December 1998, as you know. Today—nearly 3 years later—we have located a total of 16 vessels that display varied characteristics," explained Giorgi. "On the basis of both the investigative findings and the associated materials recovered, these ships can be dated from the end of the first century BC to the late fifth or early sixth century AD. Eight vessels are nearly fully intact. These include the remains of three cargo ships, three boats that were probably used on the river, one oared vessel, and the remains of one ship discovered in an upside-down position. Most of the other wrecks have been located by probes, but are not yet in the excavation stage. Still others have been individualized by numerous pieces of planking and timbers. One example of this is the so-called Hellenistic ship."

THE HELLENISTIC SHIP

Researchers had systematically labelled the ancient ships as they came to light, beginning with A. Unlike the others, however, the Hellenistic ship had been given a name.

"There were artifacts and pieces of wood scattered throughout the southern extension of the excavation site," explained Giorgi. "But unlike the other areas we did not find any complete or partially intact vessels and, therefore, had no reason to assign a project letter. Only later, when the wood fragments were cleaned and the various objects were studied did we realize that all of this material belonged, more than likely, to a single ship. The materials and wood dated to a later period than that located in other sectors of the dig and were primarily Greco-Italia [referring to the period in which Greek and Roman cultures merged], and Punic [the ancient region of Carthage, in northern Africa], in nature. [This time in history—323 to 31 BC—encompasses the last phase in historical Greek art, and is commonly known as the Hellenistic period.] Therefore, this vessel took the name 'Hellenistic ship.'"

From the initial archaeological reports, we can gain insight into the general conditions of each ship and the landscape in which they were found. In the southern extension of the excavation site, for instance, numerous planks were recovered, suggesting that they were once part of a Hellenistic craft. The discovery of this ship was a particularly dramatic event for researchers, as the presence of human bones was also found. These, along with the remains of the cargo, suggest that some of the sailors lost their lives during the destruction of the seagoing craft.

> The vessel, judging from the timbers—an intact specimen would probably measure over 2 meters in length —and planks recovered, was very large. The cargo, consisting of a vast number of amphorae of different types but predominantly Greco-Italic and Punic, most of which are intact or cracked, was found and recovered up against the remains of the nearby, ancient pier. The onboard equipment comprises a comparatively small amount of black-glazed pottery, most of which was produced at Volterra; two black-glazed lamps; two *lagynoi* [glass or ceramic containers, commonly used in ancient kitchens]; a few ointment jars both striped and plain; two painted vases of Iberian manufacture; four *thymiateria* [perfume burners], from the Punic area, probably used by the sailors for religious purposes; and part of a large gold fibula of the Celtic type. While this set of items would suggest a date in the early decades of

the second century BC, the items more intimately connected with exquisitely private practices, such as the
thymiateria, suggest that the sailors, and hence the ship,
may have been from the Punic area, and in all proba-
bility from Carthage itself [the ancient city-state in
northern Africa founded by the Phoenicians]. This
would appear to also be supported by the examination
of the animal bones found together with the amphorae. While some of these must be connected with
food for the crew, the remains of three horses and an
adult lioness must instead be regarded as associated
with cargo. In particular, the case of the lioness, whose
presence onboard can be certified on a later sarcopha-
gus lid now in the Villa Medici in Rome, supports the
hypothesis that the ship set sail from the African coast
and reached Pisa by following a route with stops along
the coasts of Sicily and Campania.

"The size of the excavation site has imposed, and will
impose in the future, problems calling for the adoption of
new solutions," explained Giorgi. "The major difficulty in
the recovery of the ships has been the vast quantity of material that accompanied each craft. Cargoes, rigging, a sailing
mast, and other material related to ancient maritime activi-

ties required detailed, time-consuming, but very important work—in particular with regards to the preservation of the wood, to avoid rapid decay."

SHIP A

The first vessel to be found, ship A, is a cargo ship that extends into a section beyond the boundaries of the current area of operation. Approximately half of the vessel, therefore, remains buried, while the wood of the exposed portion has been removed for preservation and study. Researchers are unable, at this point, to say when the ship will be fully recovered, because the extension of the excavations in the northeasterly direction, where ship A is located, has yet to be approved. Among the logistical problems is the presence of the original sheet piling placed by railway construction workers, which cut this ship in two. While an unfortunate event, the sectioning of the ship is what led to the discovery of the ancient vessels.

Ship A, according to archaeological records, stretches for about 15 meters starting from the stern. Although the keel has not yet been recovered, researchers have suggested the overall length of this vessel to measure about 30 meters. Planking and framing, connected by wooden pegs, varying in size, have been found, as have the bronze nails used in uniting the ship's construction materials. Wrote one archaeologist in the official records:

> There is no trace of its cargo, which must have been salvaged immediately after it sank in accordance with a practice that was widespread in the ancient world. Some bricks and tiles, probably belonging to the storeroom, as well as a large, worked limestone rock with holes filled with lead, perhaps a reused stone anchor, have been recovered. A few items directly connected with the vessel and an examination of the stratigraphy of the area make it possible to assign this wreck to the period after the first few decades of the second century. The state of preservation of this wreck appears to be exceptionally good, with the bulwarks and frame system perfectly preserved in their entirety.

The recovery of ancient Greco-Roman vessels, like San Rossore's ship A, is not unique, even in landlocked areas. After all, as Professor Andrew Wallace-Hadrill, director of the British School of Rome, points out, "The Romans controlled the Mediterranean as if it were a lake. They called it Mare Nostrum, Our Sea, and these ships show the range of goods that were being traded in a culturally diverse area."

In 1864, a Roman cargo ship was recovered in the ancient Greco-Roman port area of Marseille. It dated from the second or third century AD. Two large barges—measuring 70 meters long and 20 meters wide—that were constructed by Emperor Caligula for ceremonies on Lake Nemi, outside of Rome, were also recovered in recent times. Unfortunately, both ships were completely destroyed in the brutal exchange of bombs and artillery shells as the Allied forces advanced on Rome in May 1944, driving Nazi troops northward.

Similarly, between 1958 and 1965, five Roman vessels were recovered from an excavation at Fiumicino, an area next to Rome's Leonardo da Vinci Airport. These ships were harbored in the ancient Port of Claudius, much like those of Pisa, between 46 and 400 AD, and met their fate through a combination of abandonment and dramatic sea and climatic conditions. Today, the recovered vessels are part of the Museum of Roman Ships at Fiumicino.

In the 1980s, there were also two ships from the first century BC excavated from the Valle Ponti near Comacchio, along the Adriatic coast of northeastern Italy. During this same period, one of the most dramatic maritime discoveries—the largest ever, prior to the Pisa—was made during the construction of Piazza Jules Verne, upon what was obviously an ancient port, in the center of Marseille. Ten vessels, spanning a period from the fourth century BC to the sixth century AD were ultimately recovered from this site.

There was also a fifth-century ship from the Christian era recovered in the Italian city of Ravenna, during the winter of 1998. While this craft, situated next to the mausoleum of Teodorico, was making local news, workers across the Italian peninsula were driving sheet pilings at the San Rossore construction area—the same pilings that would dissect ship A and lead researchers to the maritime site of the century.

Most ancient ship excavations are found at sea. The fact that the Pisa ships are land-based makes this a unique, almost one-of-a-kind maritime archaeological project. The second aspect that sets this discovery apart from others is the quantity of the vessels and recovered artifacts. Nowhere has such a treasure trove of maritime history been found.

SHIP B

From the archive of documentation within the Co.Idra files, I pulled the file on ship B, located in area 3 of the excavation, along the northeast border, and read:

> Of the cargo ships, the oldest appears to be that nearest the remains of the ancient wharf. Thus far a section measuring 9.5 meters in length has been unearthed.

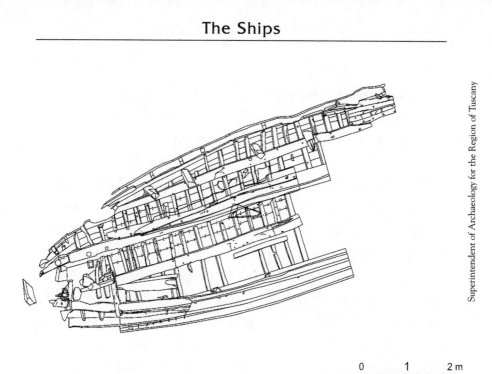

Superintendent of Archaeology for the Region of Tuscany

0   1   2 m

Ship B, located in the northeast section—area 3—of the excavation site

The ship is 4.3 meters wide and lies in the sand. It is interesting that a portion of its cargo remains intact, shifting only slightly during the sinking process. This comprises a series of amphorae laid in staggered rows one on top of the other.

The broadsides are characterized by double planking and the vessel is constructed of elements bound with mortise and tenons, which are made stronger with wooden pegs. The planking has been preserved by a natural vegetable resin used to waterproof the natural timbers and seal joints between planks.

Most of the cargo of ship B consisted of amphorae, probably manufactured in the Adriatic area. Some of these ancient "jars" contained fruit and nuts (walnuts, chestnuts, peaches, cherries, and plums), others olives, and a few specimens held sand. The analyses carried out on the content of the latter have identified the sand as the sanidine-augite type, probably from the southern Italian region of Campania. Ancient Romans used this as a degreasing agent in the production of pottery and/or bricks, even though we cannot rule out of the possibility of its use in the gymnasiums in cities like Pompeii and Herculaneum.

The report also explained that other materials found in some amphorae specimens would appear to indicate subsequent reuse, which could also account for the presence of amphorae produced in different periods on the same ship:

The material used to wedge the amphorae, constituted by small pieces of tufa stone, fragments of marble statues and small blocks and cubes of Vesuvian lava, in addition to that used to composite the ballast itself, which presents a great variety of stones, would suggest that the cargo came from the Gulf of Naples.

Many of the recovered items directly connected with the ship are associated with life onboard. These include vases in "*terra sigillata*" [a local clay], some with the names of their owners scratched on the base, and thin-walled wares, as well as lamps, glass beakers, leather and wooden objects, and coins, items which make it possible to date the vessel to early in the reign of Augustus.

The other amphorae identified in the wreck are of Spanish origin, and include Dressel 9 specimens used to contain preserved fish and fish sauces, products from the coasts of the Strait of Gibraltar in the province of Baetica that enjoyed large-scale distribution in markets throughout the Roman world. The other two specimens are again from Baetica (Haltern 70). The inscriptions most commonly found on such amphorae indicate that they were generally used to contain defrutum, a specially treated wine that could be used to preserve olives. The production of both types began at the end of the first century BC.

Considering the array of artifacts as well as ships, what priorities did researchers establish in regards to their scientific excavations? Was it more important to remove the remaining cargoes or focus efforts on the ships? Shedding some light on this area, Debora Giorgi explained that, "The stratigraphic excavation and the first preservation operations on the wooden structures proceeded in parallel, in order to avoid the loss of data and information in either field, but especially in order to preserve these delicate structures. We have therefore imposed the need to put the crafts in fiberglass 'cages,' a kind of shell that allows them to be easily moved to environments that are expressly prepared for procedures of definitive restoration."

During the summer of 2001—slightly less than 3 years after the first Roman ship was found in Pisa—the vessel labelled F was completely removed from the San Rossore site and transferred to a nearby warehouse that had been con-

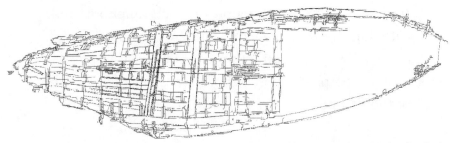

Archaeologist's design of ship C

Superintendent of Archaeology for the
Region of Tuscany/Co.Idra

verted to a naval restoration facility. It could take up to a year or more to fully bring ship F to a state in which it would be safe to place it on permanent display, most likely in the ship museum in Pisa. In the meantime, researchers work diligently on the next vessel scheduled to be removed from the excavation site, ship C.

Ship C

Ship C was found in the southernmost section of the ancient harbor. While there was some original speculation that a storm and dramatic water currents had caused this ship to sink, as digging began, a more realistic theory arose. Researchers explained that the vessel lies off the first-century wharf, about 13 meters to the west, and apparently sank while moored to a large post that was recovered alongside the vessel. According to the archaeological report:

> . . . The mooring line was still secured by a knot to a large iron ring attached to one side of the post near the top.
>
> The ship measures 11.7 meters in length and 2.8 meters in width in the middle, and retains all its structural elements (keel, keelson, timbers, dunnage, mast partners and step, top of bulwarks, and prow bollards),

as well as six rowing benches set at regular intervals. The broadsides are characterised by simple planking bound with mortise and tenons, which are made stronger with wooden pegs of different sizes. The few nails used are mostly iron.

Externally the bulwarks appear to be reinforced with two precisely squared gunwales running parallel above the quick-work. Originally protected at the edges by leather and secured with numerous bronze rivets, the apertures along the bulwarks were for the oars. The [front of the ship, or] prow is fitted with a cutwater [a device that ran along the forward edge of the vessel], and it was probably fitted with a ram or similar metal object, which was most likely salvaged in antiquity. The ship is in an extraordinarily fine state of preservation; in fact it retains large patches of red or red ochre paint applied in ancient times over a coat of white lead.

While there are not many elements serving to assign this vessel to a precise chronological period, the few items found inside the hull in the part near the prow suggest a date in the reign of Augustus, the first Roman emperor (27 BC–14 AD). This is partly borne out by the presence of Dressel 2–4 amphorae of a quite highly evolved type in the layers covering the vessel.

The areas around ship C have yielded an abundance of heterogeneous material: some bones manufacts, some lamps, fragments of glass beakers, vases in *terra sigillata*, many ropes of different size, portions of mats and leather, what is probably a wooden capstan—which extended from the deck and was used to wind the anchor cord—complete with cables, and a punched coin of an uncertain mint of Bithynia. The hole transforms the coin into an object to be hung, as an ornament, piece of jewellery, or as a talisman or charm.

Ship D

From the same report, I learned that in the northwest sector of the excavation another wreck was located, this one made of oak and found in an upside-down position.

The vessel is about 14 meters in length and has a maximum width of about 6 meters. It has a complex structure, being fitted on the sides in the vicinity of the stem and stern with pairs of projecting structures. These are set on large brackets attached above a parallel series of three beams, probably connected with the mast-stays. The broadside is characterized by a double

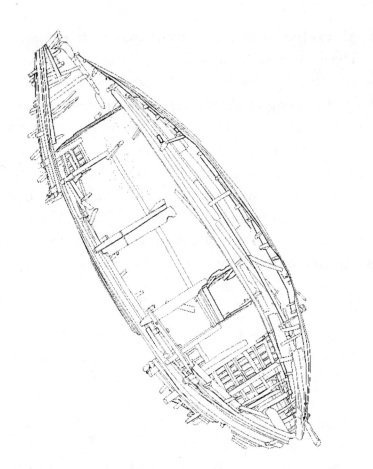

Superintendent of Archaeology for the Region of Tuscany

0   1   2 m

One of the largest and best preserved vessels discovered in Pisa is that labelled ship D, found in the northwest section—area 5—of the site.

layer of planking, or timber strips. The external bulwarks, that is, the extension of the ship's sides above the deck, are reinforced with a double gunwale, or upper edge, separated by series of planking above the waterline. The slanted prow still retains parts of an iron facing, suggesting that the tip was armed with a rostrum or similar metal-clad structure.

The central part of the keel, the garboard, the strake, and part of the adjacent planking must have been salvaged in antiquity. The vessel retains the bilge and the deck, apparently fitted only at the stern and the prow. The ship must have had a large central mast —the lower part of which has been identified—set in a socket made in one of the beams of the hull and anchored with cables to the ends of the lower posts, located below the foreparts.

A probe carried out in a sector in the center of one of the broadsides suggests that the part between the two foreparts at stem and stern is fitted with a superstructure, a sort of deckhouse consisting of arched planking attached to the top edge of the bulwarks in such a way as to continue its profile towards the interior of the vessel.

While the excavation of this last wreck is still

incomplete, the ship appears to constitute a unique example. Only comparative study with vessels from other periods will make it possible to establish its function more precisely.

On the one hand, certain structural features suggest it was used to transport foodstuffs in large terracotta [amphorae with heavy, circular lids known as] *dolia*, no trace of which has yet been found, or other exceptional cargo such as blocks of quarry stone. On the other [hand], the restricted height of the hold (just over 1 meter), the total absence of any items of cargo, and the presence of the foreparts appear to support the hypothesis that it was originally used for other purposes, and may belong to the naval tradition of another sphere.

While the report was quite detailed regarding the physical evidence presented by ship D, it was puzzling that it did not reveal any reference to the date of the vessel. By placing it into a historical content, one might more easily draw conclusions and comparisons to similar naval units. Giorgi pointed out, however, that, "At present there are no reliable chronological points of reference for this vessel, which also differs from the others in terms of building technique. The items recovered so far from the levels associated with the vessel include pottery ranging from the early Augustan age to after the Antonine era, and provide no useful insight into a specific date."

When researchers state that the San Rossore excavations could continue for decades, there are some—particularly politicians seeking a rapid conclusion to the project—who underestimate the extension of this find, both horizontally and vertically. As if to prove this point, archaeologists using

Superintendent of Archaeology for the Region of Tuscany/Co.Idra

The upside-down remains of ship D, during the initial stages of excavation

probes have discovered what appear to be the remains of two additional ships, below the upside-down remains of ship D. Given the fact that it can take up to two or three years to remove each ship, these three vessels alone could account for a decade or more of labor.

The new discoveries under ship D will undoubtedly shed additional light on the events that befell Pisa's ancient Porto delle Conche, but they may also aid researchers in targeting a date for the original vessel.

"Information of a certain interest [in regards to dating ship D]," said one researcher, "has been furnished by a few potsherds brought to light by probes that identified the two boats lying beneath the vessel, especially a small amphora of the spatheia type, which appears to suggest a date no earlier than the late fifth century."

SHIP E

A short distance from ship B, to the north, the second cargo vessel (ship E) of the San Rossore excavations was discovered laying on a sharp incline. The list of cargo that had been recovered from this ship, both inside and outside the bulwarks, reads like an inventory and, in some respect, I realized that it was. The report began:

The cargo appears to consist primarily of Dressel 2–4

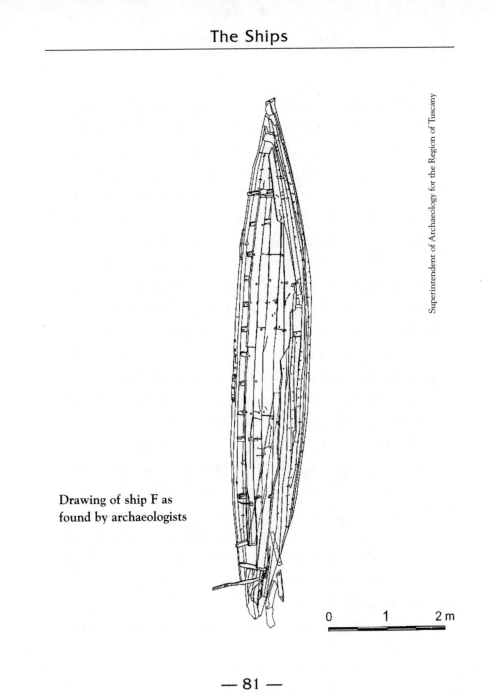

Drawing of ship F as
found by archaeologists

Superintendent of Archaeology for the Region of Tuscany

0   1   2 m

amphorae produced in Tarraconensis, Dressel 7–11 and Dressel 9 amphorae, and amphorae of the Beltran II B type from the Betic area. [A]lso recovered are a large number of hand-made impasto mugs, which would suggest that the ship—or its crew—was from the southern Gallia, fragments of the lids and walls of dolia, some lamps, bone manufactures, ceramic balsam oil flasks, terra sigillata, glasses, surgical and pharmaceutical instruments, objects in wood such as combs and a coin. There was a tradition in Roman times of placing coins under the mast step for apotropaic purposes—to ward off ill fortune and bring the voyage to a good end. [Perhaps this accounts for the single coin in this location, although there have been a number of metal coins found throughout the excavation site.]

Exposure to the dynamic movement of the waves from the northwest side of the seabed must have led to items of cargo being scattered over a large area, as is shown by the fragments of a number of glass beakers. It is therefore essential to proceed with the utmost caution in the study and interpretation of the various fragments discovered both adjacent to and in the vicinity of the wreck.

Although the data are necessarily incomplete, the

items appear to form a chronologically consistent set and make it possible to suggest a date for the cargo within the first thirty years of the first century of the Christian era.

A large wooden anchor, decorated on the shaft with a large heart-shaped leaf in relief and resembling the specimen from a ship of Lake Nemi in size as well as form, should perhaps also be attributed to this ship.

SHIP F

In the same vicinity as ships B and E (area 3) was the boat labelled F. This craft had always interested me. It is relatively narrow, slightly more than 1 meter, and measures 8.2 meters in length, and lays on its side, partly on top of ship E.

It resembles a large canoe. The particular structure of this craft—long, slim, with straight sides and raised ends—made it easy to visualize its use as a swift-flowing boat, carrying passengers or locally produced merchandise through the rivers and lagoons.

"The few items found so far in the levels of sand covering ship F and the immediate vicinity," Giorgi told me, "do not provide sufficient evidence to determine the exact purpose of the craft. Additionally—and unlike the wrecks that occupy this same excavation area—the findings provide no real proof for which it is possible to assign the boat to the first decades of the second century."

SHIP G

In the northeast corner of the San Rossore site, lying over part of ship B, is a small, 8-meter-long flat-bottom boat. Archaeologists thus far have revealed only a tiny point of this vessel, but artifacts recovered from the associated layers suggest the ship stems from the first or second century.

Co.Idra's documentation on this boat indicates that, "While the early stage of investigation makes it impossible to dwell at length on the typological and technical aspects, the vessel appears to be one of the earliest examples of a type of boat commonly used, with local variations, in the internal and the lake country of northwest Tuscany and on the Arno and the Serchio [rivers] right up to the present day."

SHIP H

Just above ship G lay the ruins of another vessel (ship H) that has been excavated in the sandy layers covering the mixed cargoes of ships B and E. The fact that a number of vessels—at least five to date—fill the same general area (area 3) of the excavation site has added to the difficulty of researchers trying to sort the pieces of this archaeological puzzle. It is almost as if maritime history has accumulated here, layer upon layer, while the harbor currents mixed and mingled the various cargoes.

Picking up the final documentation, regarding ship H, I read:

> The vessel, which appears to be of no great size, was found completely upside down and with the planking of its sides partially displaced, possibly the result of operations carried out in ancient times to salvage part of the keel, the garboard, and the strake. Although excavations have been underway only for a short time, the material found in the sand covering the side of the vessel appears to provide evidence for a dating similar to that proposed for the flat-bottomed boat, ship G.

While archaeologists labored to bring to light the first 9 of 16 ships known to exist within the San Rossore excavation, and their cargoes, another group of scientists was conducting parallel research to map out the ancient waterways of Pisa. Utilizing a combination of science and modern technology, the geomorphological evolution of the Pisan lowlands slowly emerged, including the now-extinct Auser River.

What geographical phases had this region experienced

over the past 2,300 years? How had the waterways been altered? How had the local populations utilized the rivers, the backwaters, and the sea to their advantage?

Opposite: Sketch of two anchors found at the San Rossore dig site

CHAPTER FOUR

ANCHORS & MARITIME ARTIFACTS

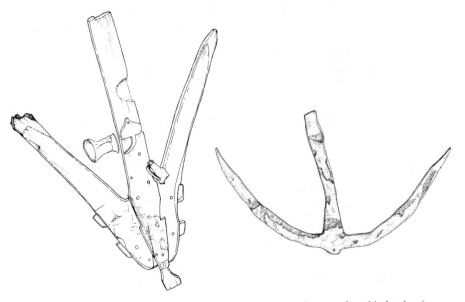

Superintendent of Archaeology for
the Region of Tuscany/Co.Idra

In museums and archaeological sites, I had seen ancient stones manipulated to fit the needs of various populations. The Neanderthal excavations in the Murcia Province of southeastern Spain had revealed stone items, dating back 50,000 years, used for cutting and cooking. On the island of Malta, there had been carved stones at Hagar Qim used for rituals as well as for hunting, felling trees, and food preparation. At the 4,000-year-old metallurgy center found on Cyprus, archaeologists had discovered rocks converted to millstones, pestles, and hammerheads. But as I toured the restoration efforts taking place around the Pisa ships, one object struck me as particularly odd: it was a rock with a series of holes in it.

"It's an anchor," came a voice from behind, as if to answer my unspoken question.

"Oh, of course," I replied, turning to meet the smile of one of the archaeologists, while at the same time laughing at myself for not seeing the obvious. Frequently the archaeologist's job is just that: seeing objects for what they are, rather than attempting to make them something they are not.

On second look, there was no doubt: it was clearly an anchor.

Apart from the raw materials and design used in ancient ship construction, one of the most important aspects was the anchor. These holding devices were so important that literary references and shipwreck excavations have indicated that it was not uncommon for a vessel to have 2 or as many as 11 aboard. It came as no surprise then—particularly with 16 ships so far—when 3 anchors emerged from the San Rossore site.

The largest and probably oldest of the ancient holding devices was the limestone rock that I had been observing. It was tapered at the edges and contained three external holes, measuring from 3 to 9 centimeters in diameter. These, I learned, were essential for attaching mooring ropes as well as to facilitate contact with the seabed. Archaeologists Barbara Ferrini and Carlotta Bigagli, responsible for the study of shipboard artifacts, were able to shed additional light on this find.

"The first anchors were stones, whose only common characteristics were sufficient weight and a naturally narrow section where the rope was to be attached. From these first examples evolved a coarsely worked stone, rounded, triangular, or trapezoidal in form [such as that found at San Rossore], and equipped with a hole at one end through which the mooring ropes passed. This type of anchor was no more than a weight offering no means of attachment to the seafloor."

From area 2 came an iron device that more closely resembles our contemporary concept of an anchor, despite its estimated first- or second-century AD date. Composed of a rectangular trunk that widens above, and two symmetrical, quarter-circle flukes with flattened hooks sharpened by a chisel or similar tool, this anchor had become greatly oxidized by time and natural elements. The anchor measures 68 centimeters in height, and has a 70-centimeter hook span.

The third anchor is a large wooden object of which only the trunk remains. This is decorated with a heart-shaped leaf. The preserved section of the broken shank measures 2.85 meters, while the maximum length at the peaks of the arms is 2.2 meters. Attached by four pegs to the shank, the arms are in an excellent state of preservation.

Anyone who has had experience aboard ships, particularly those craft powered by sail, knows that the anchor is merely one of many objects among the so-called tackle. Archaeologists working in Pisa also began to realize this as, day after day, emerged objects like blocks, tools, seamen's kits of needles, or weights for nets. So vast were the finds, in fact, that researchers chose to divide them into three groups: navigational items, shipboard tools, and shipboard furnishings.

Several objects in the first category emerged from area 2, including rigging. Area 4 produced tools that belonged to sailors, as well as a wooden block and pulley. Other objects included iron boat hooks, pottery used as weights, and a variety of bronze and iron needles that were commonly needed to mend sails and nets.

Among the array of items discovered, I was intrigued immediately upon seeing the block-pulley. Its complexity in construction, and yet simplicity of operation, seemed beyond what I had anticipated from the ancient Romans. Then again, I was quickly learning that these historical seagoers were responsible for many of the items commonly used in sailing even today.

"[The pulley consists of a] simple block made of wood with two parts fitting together to form a chest and pulley— in perfect alignment, thanks to a mounting that spins around an independent axis," Bigagli said. "The upper part, pulley, and groove have been shaped so as to allow the ropes to pass more easily. When this block was found, a rope was still preserved in its external groove, held from above by a strap, while the running-rope of the pulley was missing. In the block's upper part, there are two holes, which pass parallel to each other, through which a rope of narrower diameter was inserted, to fix the block to the mast, so as to lessen vibration."

The Hellenistic ship contained numerous shipboard tools:

three weights, used for nets, were recovered, as well as a lead weight for fishing. Here, too, was excavated a small plate in sheet bronze. Because of its design—rectangular with a central hole—researchers believe this could have been a decorative plaque.

Shipboard furnishings found in the area include an L-shaped, bronze-hinged clasp and an iron key.

While her colleagues explored the items of shipboard life, archaeologist Giuditta Grandinetti focused her studies on the many finds made from vegetable fibers: for example, matting, bags, baskets, brushes, and cord. It is unique to find fragments of this type in an excavation site because the natural fibers are highly perishable and require just the right conditions for preservation: a dry, desert setting or a wet environment, such as found in Pisa.

Grandinetti explained that, "From a technical standpoint, the working with vegetable fibers shows no substantial modification over the years, the constant recurrence of common techniques being observed even after a span of several centuries. For this reason and the lack of firm evidence linking the ships' cargoes to the vegetable-fiber artifacts, the latter were examined as a whole with no regard to chronological considerations. Moreover, the specimens found in the cargo of the [so-called] lion ship (three bags, a basket, various pieces of matting, and a large quantity of remains associated with cordage) present no technical and morphological differences with respect to those found in the vicinity of vessels dating from as much as 2 or 3 centuries later. The various areas of excavation—[the northeast sector of the site, including wrecks A, B, E, F; and the central section, ship C]—have yielded different percentages of vegetable-fiber artifacts. While most of the containers are from the northeast sector, and a considerable amount of the cordage from the central sector, no remains have yet been found inside or in the immediate vicinity of ship D."

Of particular interest are what appear to be two covers produced by twig-weaving and used to fit over glass wine flasks. This theory has emerged based, primarily, on their physical forms (thin necks that expand outward into round, almost ball-like shapes). Grandinetti and her colleagues are cautious about calling these items flask covers, since there have been no glass-and-straw wine containers documented as yet from the Roman period. Convex-bottomed glassware items, to which these would belong, are found in the Middle Ages, documented at the Crypta Balbi and the convent of San Silvestro in Genoa. From the fourteenth century onward there are also iconographic resources to these types of containers.

This does not, however, prevent archaeologists from speculating—which is without a doubt one of the more intriguing aspects of the job.

Opposite: The Mediterranean coast and inland areas around Pisa, as it may have appeared during the Roman period

CHAPTER FIVE

PISA'S ANCIENT WATERWAYS

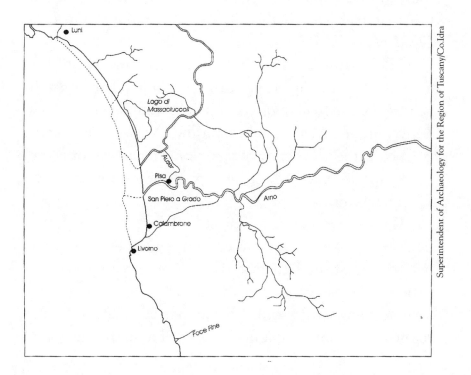

Superintendent of Archaeology for the Region of Tuscany/Co.Idra

tanding on the flat, pasturelike land alongside the San Rossore excavation site, Pisa's Leaning Tower and cathedral in the distance, it was hard to envision what the area was like some 2,000 years earlier. Was it possible to be transported back in time to, say, 250 BC? Would I find myself swimming in water deep enough to float cargo vessels or ceremonial barges? And through the transition of centuries, would I witness the various stages that led to the total cancellation of the rivers and backwaters that had created the city's once thriving Porto delle Conche?

These questions, and others, had been presented to Pasquino Pallecchi, a member of the Superintendent of Archaeology for the Region of Tuscany staff. Calling upon Marco Benvenuti and Mario Sagri, from the Department of Earth Science at the University of Florence, a team was formed to study and document the geomorphologic evolution of the Pisan lowlands.

"The discovery of the Roman vessels in the Pisan lowlands poses several problems concerning the geological and paleoenvironmental characteristics of the area under excavation and the events directly responsible for the presence of such remains," they wrote in an official report. "In this regard, important insight may be gained from the analysis of sedimentary successions and their evolution in the context of the coastal plain in which they are located."

The modern-day city of Pisa sits in a valley that opens to the sea to the west. To the northeast are the so-called Mountains of Pisa. Along the south and southeast are the Hills of Pisa and Leghorn. In the center of this geographical landscape are the Pisa lowlands, extending west to east along a 40-kilometer stretch of the River Arno and running 20 kilometers north to south along the coast. For centuries floods have come and gone here, expanding to create rivers, lakes, and marshlands, and altering the physical aspects of the Tyrrhenian shoreline.

From the geological report prepared by the reseach group, I was provided insight into the developing aspects of this region, from the Upper Miocene (10 million BC) period through the sixteenth century, shedding light not only on the physical landscape, but offering possible causes for the San Rossore shipwrecks.

The Pisa lowlands, in general, form a sedimentary basin that developed nearly 10 million years ago as a result of the same dramatic tectonic subsidence that created the northern Apennines. Since that time, continental and marine sediment deposits, estimated to be nearly 2,000 meters deep, have accumulated in this basin. According to experts, a

marine intrusion, during the Quaternary period (the Pleistocene epoch, starting about 1.6 million years ago), left
deposits of sand and silt in the region. Many of these can still
be seen along the western margins of the plain. Eventually,
as centuries passed and the sea level dropped, sandy beaches
were produced and seabeds were ultimately transformed into
coastal environments. During the Middle Pleistocene age,
this environment joined the continental landmass as pebble
and river sand deposits merged. In the last 120,000 years, at
the start of the Upper Pleistocene epoch, the area experienced at least two major fluctuations in sea level. Researchers speculate that these were caused by "global eustat-
ic and climatic events that coincide with the last two
glaciations—when the circumpolar ice sheets expanded, particularly from the arctic regions toward lower latitudes, significantly lowering sea level (to 120 meters below the present level during the last ice age)."

As in all geological evolution, changes within the Pisan
lowlands took place in stages. Between 100,000 and 10,000
years ago, for example, scientific studies indicate that the sea
level rose dramatically, moving sedimentation and altering,
once again, the landscape. Over the last 10,000 to 5,000
years, another stage occurred as the zone turned from a continental to a coastal environment with beaches, lagoons,

rivers, and lakes. It would seem that this phase of evolution continued throughout the last 2 to 3 millennia, during which time early settlements, one of which would eventually become Pisa, began to appear along the waterways.

"So far," explained the three-man research team, "the data collected from excavations and other subterranean investigations permit a stratigraphic reconstruction of the uppermost 10 meters of sediment in the area of the San Rossore site. About 3 meters of sand rest on relatively thick clay deposits not yet reached by the excavations but known from core samples, whose precise chronology and paleoenvironmental implications cannot yet be determined. These sands in turn lie under about 2 meters of alternating sand and silt deposits in the northward-slope layers [of the excavation site] containing the shipwrecks and other archaeological deposits."

While this information was interesting, and I could easily envision how the geographical surroundings could have created vast flooding over thousands of years of rising and falling sea levels, it did not, other than indirectly, provide an answer to the disappearance of the River Auser and the Porto delle Conche. Additionally, I questioned how humanity might have altered the wetlands in and around Pisa. While the climatic-eustatic dynamics over the past 15,000 years played a dominant role in the evolution of this land, human activities, as illustrated throughout history, must have caused environmental change that, in turn, influenced the area's hydrographic past.

"The environment and geographical nature of the area in which the settlement of Etruscan and Roman Pisa was born and developed is now very different from what it was in ancient times," explained San Rossore Project Director Stefano Bruni. "This is due to the abandonment of the defenses connected with the centuriate system, the rising sea level, and the hydrological deterioration produced by the political, economical, and demographic crises undergone by the city in late ancient times, as well as subsequent radical reclamation projects undertaken from the Middle Ages onward."

Examples of such reclamation efforts can be found in the recent excavations at San Rossore. Among the shipwrecks and artifacts, archaeologists, in the more surface levels, also recovered vast quantities of construction materials related to life in and around the harbor. Some examples include mosaic pavement, walls that had been decorated with frescos, stuccoes, marble, and even statuary, which, according to researchers, were frequently discarded during restorations.

Because these materials found their way into the waters of the ancient harbor, it has been speculated that certain city structures—probably beginning during the Imperial Age—were demolished and, because of its closeness and convenience, dumped into the port. This theory is also supported by scientific excavations in recent years carried out around Pisa's Bell Tower in Piazza del Duomo. Here, less than 500 meters from the ancient Porto delle Conche, archaeologists found that, from the fifth century onward, buildings in this area had been removed for the development of a city cemetery.

There exists little information on the hydrography of the Pisan area as a whole. However, dumping of construction debris is one example of how historical populations may have assisted in the alteration of the surrounding harbor structure. This practice, combined with flooding—a major problem along the Arno even today—which brought with it loads of silt from both rivers as well as the nearby sea, created change in the regional landscape. This rapid silting of the harbor was also responsible for quickly covering the ships that are now being excavated and preserved.

"While glimpses of the course of the Auser [River] in ancient times are offered solely by a series of geomorphologic surveys and photographic interpretations," said Bruni, "that of the Arno [we have proven] differed substantially from its present situation. Of the three branches mentioned by [Greek writer] Strabo, apart from the one coinciding with the present course, it is possible to identify only the south-ernmost branch."

As part of their studies, and in an effort to determine the flow of major waterways—the Arno and the Auser Rivers—in historical Pisa, researchers turned to technology. Utilizing remote sensing analysis and infrared scanners, they were able to map out the shifting course of ancient riverbeds buried throughout the city. The results of these studies were then matched to the few ancient charts of Pisa known to exist, including those of Leonardo da Vinci (1503) and Geromino Bellarmato (1536).

The findings revealed that the Arno had, throughout the centuries, shifted dramatically from its current course. During the time of the Porto delle Conche, in fact, the river had followed a path nearly 5 kilometers north of that found today.

Current research and a reconstruction of the Pisan waterways of the Roman period indicate the Auser River began as a tributary of the River Serchio, roughly 20 kilometers to the north, and ran in a north-to-south direction until, in Pisa, it met the Arno. The urban harbor, archaeologists speculate, was situated near this river union, in one of the bends along the Arno.

"The gradual silting up . . . [of the harbor in Roman times] . . . was probably due to the sudden massive accumulation of detritus swept along by the waters of the Auser," wrote Stefano Bruni in a report on the ancient Porto delle Conche and the waters that created it. "The basin probably shrank by a considerable number of meters and the bank must have coincided more or less with the bottleneck of the present excavation area. A considerable number of pieces of *terra sigillata* have been found at this point and at approximately the same depth as the destruction levels associated with the pier.

"As a result of the silting up of the southernmost part of the basin, new harbor structures were built in the reign of Tiberius, if not indeed in that of Claudius."

Bruni continued to explain how man's intervention into the evolutional changes of the harbor area was in direct relation to the levels and shifting of waterflows, as well as the continuous silting and filling of the port area due to storms and floods. An ancient wharf, for example, was found during the digs, comprised of rough, stone blocks of various sizes and shapes, and united by mortar. The section of the wharf currently unearthed runs southeast to northwest and measures over 8 meters in length and 1.70 meters thick. At one end of this ancient seawall, two tetragonal structures sit directly opposite one another.

I was curious about what relationship, if any, the location of this structure had in the altering of water currents and, more specifically, whether its presence, over the centuries, had altered the foundation of the harbor itself. Professor Bruni was quick to provide an answer, linked, once again, to the speculated waterflow of the urban harbor, based on archaeological findings.

"The structure lies at a much higher level than the wharf of the classical period and the pier of the Hellenistic harbor [which have also been uncovered in the excavation]. While this may be connected with the constant accumulation of sand and detritus carried along by the Auser, and especially with the phenomena that caused the southern section of the basin to silt up, its location in the easternmost area would also appear to have been an important factor. The excavations have, in fact, repeatedly revealed that, with all the natural variations caused by the movement of the waves, and with no lack of deep and sudden depressions, the various sediments deposited on top of each other on the bottom of the basin over the centuries all sharply incline to the northwest, in the direction of the coastline."

From the research team of Benvenuti, Pallecchi, and Sagri, I gathered that many of the paleogeographical changes of the area, from the Roman period forward, were revealed when the stratigraphic data was matched to San Rossore's geomorphological and historical documentation:

[During the Roman] . . . period the coastline lay about 3 to 4 kilometers west of the excavation site, and there is evidence of an ancient Roman port near San Piero a Grado, by the mouth of the Arno. It would seem that the area immediately inland from the coast was characterized by channels and stretches of water, some navigable, whose existence is documented by historic sources. A hydraulic map of the Pisan lowlands at the beginning of the sixteenth century, and generally considered a useful approximation of the ancient situation, was drawn up by Leonardo da Vinci. The San Rossore site most likely coincides with an ancient landing spot along one of these channels, which lay just north of the right bank of the Arno.

The nature of the sediments so far observed in the alternating sand and silt deposits, which have yielded the ancient material, leads one to believe that the area was repeatedly flooded, and sometimes so violently as to move the ships and disperse portions of their cargoes, though these events have not yet been dated. The ancient landing site, in fact, lay near the outer extremity of a pronounced bend in the Arno, where particularly violent floods would break levees as well as deposit sand along the riverbed. Moreover, we learn from the historical records that already in the reign of Cosimo I some of the channels by the coast created serious problems of flooding due to seastorms, whose debris tended to block the mouths of the canals and of the rivers to which they were linked. These problems, despite the sustained efforts of such eminent hydraulic engineers as Benedetto Castelli (at the close of the sixteenth century), had not yet been solved. We may plausibly suggest, then, that in times of particularly frequent and intense rains, the area was, already in antiquity, prone to floods, which called for some form of forecasting and control. It would seem, therefore, that the events responsible for the sinking and partial destruction of the San Rossore ships must have been so exceptional in their violence as to be unpredictable.

The fierce power of the open ocean during a storm is not a mystery to humans, particularly to those who live and work by the sea. But how violent could the inland waters have been in this ancient urban port? Could the rush of seawater have been so violent that it overturned and smashed these vessels, tearing their sails to shreds and spewing their cargoes along the harbor floor?

The answers to these questions, from scientists and archaeologists alike, were yes. There is no doubt that at certain times in the history of this area, dramatic flooding and other natural events that changed the geological profile of the region would have been sufficiently aggressive to have created havoc with even the strongest ship of the Classical and Roman era.

How seaworthy had the ships of Pisa been? Was it possible that poor construction had contributed to their fate?

During the Roman Empire, the coastal town of Torre del Greco, south of Naples, had thrived as one of the major shipbuilding centers of the Mediterranean. It was here that I would find the answers to my questions, and actually witness the construction of an "ancient" Roman vessel.

Opposite: Ship B, located in the northeast section—area 3—of the excavation site

CHAPTER SIX

ROMAN SHIPBUILDING

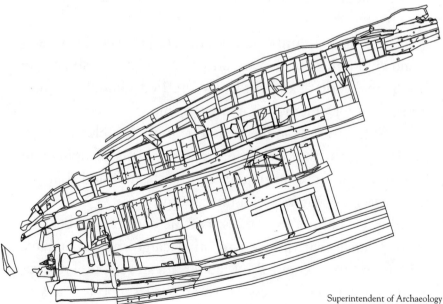

Superintendent of Archaeology
for the Region of Tuscany

In his book, *Ships and Seamanship in the Ancient World*, Lionel Casson explains that the technique and skill of Greek and Roman shipbuilders was "so refined that it more resembles cabinetwork than carpentry."

The ships of Pisa reinforce this concept, demonstrating a building technique that began with the keel and worked up, plank by plank. The collection of vessels found at San Rossore, in fact, enriched not only the knowledge of historical ship types, but contributed to the scientific community's understanding of construction methodologies employed by ancient Mediterranean craftsmen in the building of seagoing vessels.

"There are certainly unique aspects [among the vessels found in Pisa], though we cannot consider the ships rare among the world of ancient Rome," retired admiral and maritime expert Domenico Carro wrote me in an e-mail message. "Ship D, for example, is unique in the simple fact that, to date—with the exception of two remains found in Marseille—no other antique vessel has been found that has the obvious appearance of a military ship.

"Ship C is also very interesting," he continued, "because of its diversity with respect to other cargo ships that have been found throughout the Mediterranean region. This was a large, oar-powered vessel, which also supported a sail.

[Ancient shipbuilders had] fit the ship with a cutwater on the prow and a ram."

Three of the ships found in Pisa, and labelled A, B, and E, revealed a design and construction method common to cargo ships of the period between the first century BC and the late fifth or early sixth century AD (the dates spanning the origins of the Pisa ships). These were, for the most part, deep-bellied, sailing vessels with a single mast. Below the main deck were cargo holds, sectioned off for amphorae, in the aft, with other merchandise—including livestock and wild beasts, including lions that were loaded in northern Africa to be sold in Rome—being systematically stowed forward. Some craft had a "balcony" extending from the stern of the ship, while, on larger vessels, there was even a cabin on the upper deck. From here a single oarsman could navigate the ship using a long-handled paddle. In front of the mast a stairwell leading to the bowels of the ship was traditionally incorporated. Beyond that, at the prow, was a browsprit, supporting a small sail that aided in navigating the vessel. Here, too, was generally stowed the anchor.

In his scientific documentation, Professor Stefano Bruni detailed the cargoes found in and around ships A, B, and E. When discussing the latter, however, he also added a note regarding an anchor found nearby: "A large wooden anchor, decorated on the shaft with a large heart-shaped leaf in relief and resembling the specimen from the ships of Nemi in size as well as form. . . ."

Throughout my research I had heard repeated reference to the ships of Lake Nemi, a picturesque setting southeast of Rome. I had previously written a small feature on the two great ceremonial barges found there, attributed to Roman Emperor Caligula. The story focused on the efforts of an Italian businessman, Rosario D'Agata, to reconstruct a full-size replica of one of the two vessels, both of which had been completely destroyed during bombings in World War II.

I went through my archive of past research materials, pulling a dusty, gray folder titled, "Dianae Lucus." This was the association name under which D'Agata had conceived the ship reconstruction project. While there was no direct relationship between the ships of Caligula and those of Pisa, there was at least one indirect link: the vessel of the Dianae Lucus Project was to have been reproduced using the same handcrafed techniques used by ancient Roman shipbuilders. I therefore determined that by observing how the reproduced ship from Lake Nemi was built, and talking to the craftsmen involved, I would also gain a better understanding of the methodology used to construct the ancient watercraft of San Rossore.

A friendly, energetic Italian, sporting a gray beard and large glasses, D'Agata explained that the original ceremonial barge, on which the reconstruction project is based, was a colossal 70 meters long and 20 meters broad, built of oak and pine and waterproofed with wadding and lead sheeting, which was then fixed with hundreds of copper nails.

While the use of nails was not a common factor in all of the ships of Pisa, they had been found in the oak remains of ship D. This vessel had been discovered in an upside-down position in the northwest section of the dig and was missing most of its quickwork. Bruni explained that ship D, in addition to the use of iron nails, demonstrated other construction characteristics that set it apart from the others.

"Instead of the customary ancient system whereby the planks of the broadside are held together by means of mortise and tenon joints embedded in each plank and secured with a small wooden pin, the planks [of ship D] are attached to the timbers of the frame by means of iron nails. . . . Iron nails are archaeologically documented from halfway through the first century BC onwards . . .

"[The techniques used in ship D] are usually regarded as belonging to a late period. While the mortise and tenon system appears to be characteristic of both Greek and Roman naval engineering, this does not rule out the possibility that other methods began to be used in the Roman era, including both the frame and the mixed technique. This appears to be borne out by another buried wreck excavated in the 1960s at Pontana Longarini in southern Sicily and dated around 500 AD. A similar technique also appears to have been used for the early fifth-century vessel of Port Vendres."

Returning to the Dianae Lucus Project, D'Agata had said, 2 years earlier, that the ambitious effort of bringing a Lake Nemi barge back to life, in a full-size replica, would cost an estimated $7 million. All the work, he pointed out, would be done on a strictly scientific basis. In most cases, this would have left the completed ship open to controversy regarding its construction. The original vessels, however, had been in good condition prior to their destruction in May 1944, and experts had examined and studied them in great detail.

"We have a wealth of documentation to draw upon," he had explained. "We are going to begin with the forward part of the ship, including the bow and 18 meters of the keel, as there are no doubts about what that was originally like."

But how had the project progressed during the past 2 years? Had D'Agata succeeded in concluding his dream? If so, whom had he engaged to handcraft the vessel and what could I learn from them about ancient shipbuilding?

"The construction of the first section of the ship has been

completed at the Di Donato Shipyards at Torre del Greco, near Naples, which is cosponsoring this part of the reconstruction work," D'Agata told me in a phone conversation. "This is one of the last remaining yards specializing in the old traditional arts. It's ironic to think that the original ships were built here in Nemi by master shipwrights brought in by Caligula from the imperial naval base at Capo Miseno, which is just up the coast from Torre del Greco."

The completed framework of the ship was to be transported to the shores of Lake Nemi, near the Ships of Nemi Museum that once held the original vessels, where the contruction would be completed, funding permitting.

Torre del Greco housed the wooden skeleton of what would someday be the reconstructed efforts of Rosario D'Agata and the Dianae Lucus Project. The massive keel, showing dark signs of fire where the hardwood had been treated and the incisions of handcrafting tools, curved upward, ending in a loop that resembled a giant pig's tail.

Among the workers I found a veteran shipbuilder, his hands gnarled with age and marked with the scars of a carpenter. Clad in a checked, wool shirt and sporting a blue ballcap with gold letters reading "USS George Washington, CVN 73," I felt an immediate attraction to this man. He had spent most of his life working at the Di Donato Shipyards, and had participated in the construction of more ancient replicas than I had seen in 2 decades of museum hopping.

The range of people that provided input for my study of the San Rossore excavation was vast. I had spent months speaking with engineers, scientists, and scholars about the various aspects of Pisa's ancient landscape and, in particular, the 2,000-year-old vessels uncovered there. Now I listened to this shipbuilder who spoke through the smoke of a Camel cigarette about the wisdom of ancient shipbuilding techniques that had, for centuries, been passed from father to son.

"Ancient shipbuilding methods were completely different from those used today," he began. "It was not until the Middle Ages that the practice of building a skeleton—that is, putting ribs onto the keel and then fixing hull planks onto this—became popular. [This is the so-called skeleton first method of construction.] Before that, ships were built plank by plank, starting from the keel. The Greeks and Romans were masters at this 'shell first' way of making ships. Planks, in this case, were attached directly after laying the keel. The internal supports, or skeleton if you will, were added later."

But how did the planks remain in place if there was no internal support, no "bones" on which to attach them?

The aged craftsman posed his lips as if to whistle, blew a

single stream of smoke into the crisp air, then answered, "Well, son, they were fixed to each other, naturally. Along the edge of each plank—I believe 'strake' is the English term—slots were drilled. These were called 'mortises' and could be anywhere from 15 to 25 centimeters apart. On the next strake, similar holes would be drilled, corresponding to those of the previous plank. When the holes were matched up between two planks, a tiny piece of hardwood, or tenon, with two holes, would then be placed between them and locked into place with pegs or treenails.

"So, we have two stripes of planking, one on the other, and every 15 or so centimeters, we have a tenon joint. Using this method the planking became self-supporting, beginning from the keel. It was also extremely solid and ensured planking maintained the desired shape."

And what about caulking? What process sealed the ship and prevented leaks?

"The strakes used were large, sometimes 10 centimeters or more. Because of this, the joints were normally so tight that caulking was not required," he smiled, with a twinkle of wisdom in his eyes. "But we all know that something has to be applied to protect the ship from water, now don't we? In this case, the hull would have been covered with a tarred fabric, then coated in lead—to keep out the shipworms. That is not to say that caulking would never be used, particularly in small vessels."

This brought to mind a scientific report I had read regarding the ships of Pisa, which went into depth on the topic of caulking. It had, in fact, explained that in some of the ships caulking had been found both in and outside the planking, used to waterproof the wood as well as seal the joints. It was also applied to "protect the wood against biological aggression."

To protect seagoing vessels from mollusks and other hazards, a further measure was to cover the exterior of the ships with lead sheeting, held in place by copper nails. Evidence of this had been found on ship C, in the central area of the excavation site.

The report, prepared by scientists Gianna Giachi and Pasquino Pallecchi, went on to explain that:

The analyses of the organic constituents of caulking material from vessels B, E, F, and C identify it as a natural vegetable resin, most likely of pine, which has been thermally treated; either pitch, tar, or a mixture of resin and tar. A more precise identification must await the forthcoming gas-chromatographical analysis. Vessel C exhibits a small area where some reddish color is still present. The pigment is red ochre (iron oxide and mineral clay), and this red ochre seems to have been applied on top of a white coat of lead carbonate (cerussite) and basic lead carbonate (hydrocerussite). In some areas those elements were transformed into black lead sulphide (galena).

The two lead carbonates form a white pigment known to us as "white lead," and to the ancients as *cerussa*. This could be obtained artificially by exposing lead to vaporised vinegar, and then transforming acetate into carbonate through contact with the air. Pliny describes its use, together with that of other pigments, in covering ships using an encaustic painting technique: "with these same colors [among which he cites *cerussa*] was tinted for paintwork and encaustic paintings. This technique is not suited for use on walls; it is, however, commonly used for warships and even for merchant vessels."

Analysis of the pigments' binders reveals the presence of a vegetable resin, colophony, and beeswax. Pliny again confirms: "Then a third process is performed, wherein a brush is used after the wax has been melted on the fire. Paint thus applied to a ship waterproofs it against sun, salt, and wind."

On ship E's external planking there is evidence not only of caulking, but also of the application of white paint containing calcium carbonate and white clay (kaolinite). Here again the binders used were a mix of colophony and beeswax. . . .

Gazing upward, toward the oak keel of the Nemi reconstruction, I wondered about construction materials. What had been the favored timber for Greek and Roman vessels, such as those of San Rossore, and why? Like almost all Neapolitans, even those living in the outlying areas such as Torre del Greco, my newfound friend had an answer.

"You must remember that shipyards were found throughout the Mediterranean. They were building ships of all types and, frequently, the selection of timber was dictated by the vessel. For instance, a warship would commonly have an oak keel that would withstand rammings. I have heard that in Pisa they also found both oar- and sail-powered merchant ships as well as a *navis oneraria*, which were commonly used for transporting wine amphorae and grain around the Mediterranean Sea. These vessels could have been constructed using a variety of wood. As a general rule, Greeks and Romans used whatever timber was locally available. It was a matter of convenience rather than necessity."

While the subject of wood might seem a minor factor to some, archaeologists and scientists involved in projects of historical nature understand the value in a piece of ancient timber. Within each fiber is documented the history from which the material stems, if only one knows the right combination to unlock this archive of ancient knowledge.

Researchers at the San Rossore excavation, fully understanding the value of wood samples, turned to Gianna Giachi of the Superintendent of Archaeology for the Region of Tuscany, to coordinate and document the identification and analysis of each specimen from the site. With the assistance of the University of Florence and the Istituto per la Ricerca sul Legno (C.N.R.), Giachi prepared an initial report, with researchers Simona Lazzeri and Stefano Paci, explaining that: "Analyses taken from the numerous finds of wooden objects, including all those from the shipwrecks found in Pisa/San Rossore excavations, have added to our knowledge of the type of timber used during the period under investigation."

The report continued, echoing the words of the aged craftsman I'd met at Torre del Greco: "Identification of the types of wood used both in various sections of the hulls and in a range of artifacts reveals choices made [by ancient shipbuilders] and the criteria behind them (durability, mechanical characteristics, and so on). Choices were, however, also influenced by the more or less ready availability of different timbers."

The Instituto per la Ricerca sul Legno (C.N.R.) froze original wood specimens in order to hand-cut thin-layer samples, following the three main anatomical directions of the wood tissue (cross, longitudinal tangential, and longitudinal radial sections). Done with care, this resulted in minimal damage to the original wood discoveries. The layers were then examined under an optical microscope to determine and compare characteristics of each wood type. The results of this and other studies could then be developed into a microxilotomic report. Giachi's report continued:

Identification of wood types began with ships B, F, C, and D. At present, when we consider just how much we have in the way of samples, thanks to the relative ease of the operation, our results may seem paltry, but we have taken them singly, one by one, as the pieces of the hulls were brought to light.

For [ships] C and D in particular, with 59 samples analyzed, [we've concluded that] coniferous wood was used for the planking, *Pinus pinaster Aiton* in the former, and *Pinus pinea L* (stone pine) in the latter.

Elsewhere in both ships, *Abies alba Miller* (silver fir) was used. Because none of these species are significantly resistant to fungi or more than slightly resistant to insect aggression unless properly treated, the vessels had been caulked [through the application of pitch]. Fir is scarcely resistant to the alternation of soaking and drying, so it is best used for quickwork.

Nowadays such timbers are not used in naval or maritime constructions, whereas both Latin and Greek authors record their use for such purposes in antiquity. Plutarch notes that the stone pine was dedicated to Poseidon "because it grows along the beaches of the sea and dunes and because it is very useful for naval construction."

The generic term "pine" is mentioned by several authors. One must bear in mind, however, that any type of resinous tree may have been designated as such. The fact remains, even so, that the fir was naturally considered the best tree for masts, because of its good, straight, and exceptionally tall trunk.

The planking of ships B and F appears to have been mainly of oak. The wood of this tree, and in particular its duramen, is very durable and resistant to insects. Along with many other uses, it is recommended for shipbuilding, where it is often used to construct the framework, the axis of the keel, the timbers, and so on because of its mechanical characteristics. In ship D holly-oak is present in the frame.

To judge from the data obtained so far, a remarkable variety of timbers seem to have been used in the frames of vessel C—eight items in fig wood, one in olive, one in ash, one in elm, and one in holly-oak. This suggests a succession of repairs.

From the preliminary results, it is surprising how much common fig wood is present. Fig is a soft wood, easy to carve and alter. It may have been used on account of its availability. Even so, this does not pin down the ship's origin to a precise geographical location. Although this species originated in North Africa, it was already widespread throughout the Italian peninsula in pre-Roman times on account of its fine fruit.

Finally, we have found that, as with other wrecks, vice cuttings—from pruning—were used as padding in the stowage of cargoes.

Each species of tree identified so far exhibits the same pattern of distribution, being generally widespread throughout the Mediterranean area and especially along the Italian coasts. Each would be readily available in the area of Pisa, which, as Strabo pointed out, owed its importance as a seaport to the abundant supply of construction timber.

In the same respect, if we consider wood alone, the refound ships of Pisa—particularly the larger vessels—could have also been constructed in one of several other ports that bordered the Mare Nostrum. This was pointed out to me by Dr. Dario Giugliano, a medical researcher and author of the recently published *The Way They Ate: Origins of the Mediterranean Diet*.

From his office at the Second University of Naples, Giugliano explained that the original Mediterranean landscape was rich and heterogeneous. The high mountains were covered with black pine and cedar. On the gentle slopes, oak faired better at withstanding the heat. Over hills and dales reigned holm oak and other broadleaf trees. Drought-resistant olive and cork trees colonized the sandstone slopes. At the shoreline, solitary maritime pine often grew skyward with wind-bent trunks.

"In classical time the woodland areas of the Mediterranean [also] underwent aggressive deforestation," said Giugliano. "Even Plato described the barren and arid hills of the southeastern extremity of central Greece (Attica), which had, by the fifth century BC, become denuded: 'What remains today is like the skeleton of a sick man, because the fertile and soft earth has eroded.'"

Dr. Giugliano explained that, "The many civilizations that flourished in this area caused great changes in the environment. The mountain conifers were cut. Shipbuilders sought their long and straight trunks. And hardwoods were destroyed for charcoal."

In addition to information on shipbuilding, my research provided a greater understanding of ancient maritime trading and the resulting mix of Mediterranean cultures. Studying the cargoes recovered from the San Rossore excavation, the complexity of Rome's historic shipping network became obvious. Carthaginian olive oil and Celtic jewelry had been found at the site, indicating that at least one of the ships may have traveled from northern Africa to Tarragona and Narbonne, prior to reaching Pisa. Recorded trade routes of the Roman Empire indicate, as well, that luxury goods and staples such as ivory from East Africa, spices and cotton from India, silk from China, and wheat, linen, and marble from Egypt were commonly carried to their final destinations by seagoing units.

Like a sailor guided by the stars, I read the reports provided by the Superintendent of Archaeology for the Region of Tuscany regarding the objects recovered at the Pisa site. There were literally tens of thousands of artifacts and items of everyday use. Each shed light on the history of the ships and, at the same time, turned my investigation toward the ancient trade routes used by the crews of these and other maritime vessels.

Opposite: Pisa played a major role in maritime trading throughout the Mediterranean Sea during the Roman period. This map illustrates some of the more popular routes made by cargo ships of this era.

1. Restoration of ship C
Following spread: 2. A nighttime view of the archeological excavations at San Rossore

3. The fiberglass-encased ship B

4. Members of the excavation crew clean off an ancient anchor.

5. The so-called "sailor and dog" skeletons found in area 2-3 of the San Rossore site

6. The visible remains of ship C, located in area 4 of the San Rossore site

7. The structure of a boat is covered with resin to protect the wood from rapid decay.

8. Upside-down, ship D is located in area 5 of the excavation site.

9. Protecting the ships as they emerge into the elements after 2000 years is a primary concern among archaeologists.

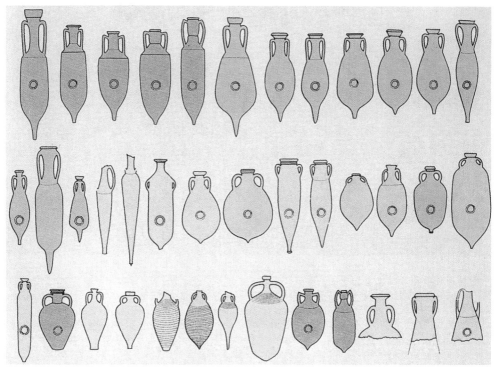

10. Roman amphorae: Republic era, 509–27 BC, in brown; 1st century AD, green; 2nd–3rd centuries AD, blue; 4th century AD, yellow

11. The visible remains of ship C, located in area 4 of the San Rossore site

12. One of three anchors found in the Pisa excavation site

13. Cargoes found near ship E

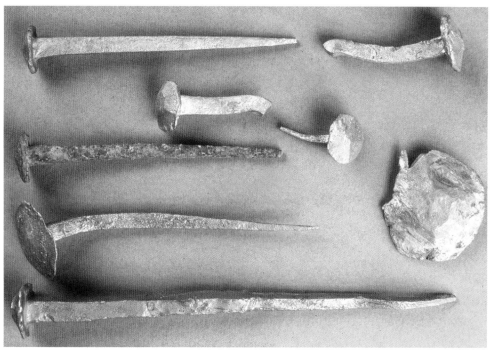

14. Nails from the vessels of the Pisa ships

15. A wooden pulley was among the shipboard remains recovered from the archaeological site.

16 & 17. Ancient Roman coins, such as this, are part of the treasure trove of artifacts.

18. A theatrical mask decorates this glass vase, dating from the 1st century BC to the 1st century AD.

18. A decorative 1st century cup or *terra sigillata*.

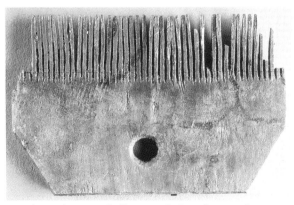

19. Several personal effects, including this wooden comb, were found by archaeologists.

20. An ancient incense burner, in the form of a female bust

This page and opposite: 21 & 22. Start of the reconstruction of a Roman ship, under Project Diana

23. A view from inside The Ancient Ships of San Rossore Museum

CHAPTER SEVEN

PISA'S HARBOR & ANCIENT MEDITERRANEAN TRADING

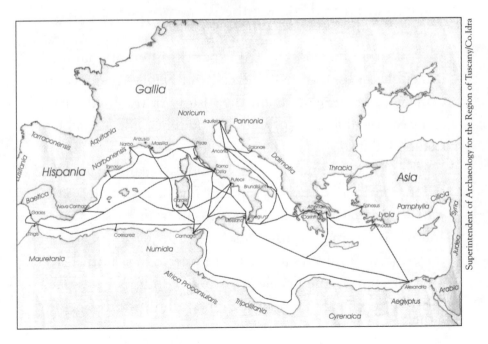

Superintendent of Archaeology for the Region of Tuscany/Co.Idra

The pieces of the archaeological puzzle were coming together. Of the 16 vessels located within the San Rossore excavation thus far, I now knew that at least three were cargo ships, used for transporting goods such as wine and grain to and from various Mediterranean ports. But how did this trio of vessels fit into the overall scheme of ancient sea trade? Where had they traveled? What had been their mission? How had they contributed to Pisa as a seaport? For that matter, what role had the city's urban harbor played in the overall picture of Mediterranean trade during the Roman Republic and Empire?

Dr. Dario Giugliano, noted expert in international medical circles at the Second University of Naples, had recently completed a 5-year study on the history of the Mediterranean Sea, including its peoples, its cultures, and its ancient trading habits.

"The Mediterranean is an inland sea, land-locked between continents," he explained. "The sea is small and its waters are relatively calm. You can sail from coast to coast, and when passing through wide-open seas with threatening waves, there is always an island to offer refuge until better weather comes. The privilege of these conditions has made the Mediterranean a unique focal point on the crossroads of civilization. Its geographic position has assured a great number of human contacts, a variety of relationships, and florid trade and culture exchange. Other, even older, civilizations such as the Chinese, advanced alone, but not the Mediterranean peoples. They were continually renewed and enriched by the blending of different cultures. Each marked the prodigious growth of Western civilization, which dominated humankind for 2 millennia."

While there is insufficient evidence to provide an exact chronology of Pisa's ancient harbor, recovered artifacts and the fact that it supported a settlement that stemmed from the end of the ninth century BC allow us to speculate that the initial urban port began nearly 800 years before Christ. Perhaps, at that time, it was no more than a backwater landing. The fact that it linked the settlement to the open sea, however, would be a key factor in the development and growth of Pisa.

The Mediterranean Sea during this early period had already been dominated by the Phoenicians for over 400 years. As Dr. Giugliano pointed out, "They invented fast ships, were shrewd, and had a sense of direction. They explored both land and sea. . . . Everywhere they went they opened markets and built ports. The black ships [of the Phoenicians] berthed at every port in the Mediterranean. . . .

By about 1100 BC they were in Tunisia and on the Atlantic coast of Spain. In the ninth century there were Phoenician settlements on Cyprus, Malta, and Sardinia; a century later they were in Sicily. . . . Merchants from Tyros had established the berth at Carthage . . . [and] by importing massive quantities of grain from Sardinia and silver from Spain, this city would become the richest in the world."

Despite its maritime superiority, Carthage frequently contested its domination of the sea with the Sicilian Greeks and, ultimately, ended up colliding with the growing Roman expansion. The Punic Wars between Rome, dominant in Italy and the northern Mediterranean, and Carthage, which controlled northwest Africa and the western Mediterranean, took place in three stages of mortal conflict that lasted more than a century (264–146 BC).

For some time Rome had negotiated with Carthage for the protection of shipping lanes between Africa and around Sicily. Because the Italian island was a valuable asset—who controlled Sicily also dominated the Straits of Messana (today Messina), the waterway between mainland Italy and Sicily—the Carthaginians occupied Messana in 264 BC, starting the First Punic War, so called for the geographical area of Rome's enemy.

Over the next 3 years, Rome would enhance its naval

forces, utilizing them and a powerful land army to drive out the southern invaders, and ultimately forcing them to surrender not only Sicily, but Corsica and Sardinia as well.

By 218 BC, Carthage had gained full control of Spain following campaigns led by Hamicar and his sons, Hasdrubal and Hannibal. When the latter captured Saguntum, an ally to Rome, the Second Punic War was declared. History books recall this war for the incredible invasion of Italy by Hannibal. Much to his enemy's surprise, Hannibal marched over the Alps with select troops and a corps of elephants, to take on, and defeat, Roman armies in three major battles.

It was the strategy of Rome, however, that finally brought Hannibal to his knees. While the Carthage leader was battling in enemy territory, brothers Gnaeus and Publius Scipio were cutting off fleet supply lines, and Scipio Africanus Major was pushing the Punic army from Spain. In 202 BC, after being recalled to protect Carthage, Hannibal was defeated at Zama by Scipio and Numidian King Messinissa, thereby ending the war.

Despite the fact that Carthage became a dependent of Rome, there were members of the Roman political and military systems that viewed the northern African city as a constant threat that must be crushed. Therefore, using a minor uprising as an excuse, Rome declared the Third, and final,

Punic War in 149 BC. According to ancient historian Poly-
bius, Carthage died without surrender. In 3 years, the city
was in rubble, and her people, once dominators of the
Mediterranean Sea, were slaves of the Romans.

In his article "Rome's Lost Ships," editor Robert Kunzig
summed up the importance of Mediterranean sea trade to
the ancient Romans this way:

> The Empire drew its strength from maritime trade, and
> the Pisa dig is a vast muddy warehouse of Roman sea-
> going details. Augustus came to power as Rome's first
> emperor in 30 BC after his fleet defeated Mark Antho-
> ny's at Actium, off western Greece, and he went on to
> establish a formidable navy to rid the Mediterranean of
> pirates. After that the Roman Sea was criss-crossed reli-
> ably by thousands of merchant ships. People in Rome, a
> city of perhaps a million, came to depend for their very
> bread on wheat from Egypt and North Africa; they
> drank wine from France, and cooked (and massaged
> themselves) with olive oil from Spain. The basic vec-
> tors of this amazingly internationalized economy are
> known from myriad documents and digs.
>
> What isn't so well known, and what these ships
> promise, is the sort of detail that makes history come

alive—details about ancient Pisa itself, about ancient ships, and about the life of an ancient harbor.

The Etruscans had originally constructed the Pisa backwater and pier, according to the San Rossore archaeological team. That being the case, the city was already several hundred years old when the Romans came along. Shortly after defeating Carthage in the Punic Wars of the third and second centuries BC, the Roman government decided that Pisa would be a perfect location, given its many inland waterways, for a naval base.

Ostia, the river port outside Rome, and Pozzuoli, to the south, constituted the two ends of the Roman harbor system during the Republic period. Adding Pisa extended this Mediterranean "docking zone" an additional 300 kilometers to the north. This, in turn, increased the importance of the city and justified the construction of inland roadways between the capital and the western port-city.

Pisa would soon become a crossroads of sea and land, offering military shelter and strategic positioning during times of war, and easy access to maritime commerce in times of peace. Despite its increasing importance, however, the city would not become a colony of Rome for over 250 years, and the rise of Augustus. From 20 BC, however, Pisa would thrive in the shadow of the empire, developing, among other public structures, a theater, baths, and numerous temples—none of which remain today.

While Pisa grew, so too did the Roman Empire, expanding its territorial reign northward into Aquitana, Germania, Belgica, and Britannia; westward as far as the Atlantic Ocean; and all of the territory east of Italy, including the modern-day Balkan Peninusla, Cyprus, the Middle East, into Egypt, and along the northern coast of Africa. A reflection of this geographical development, and the resulting sea trade, can be seen in the remains of merchandise carried by the vessels of the San Rossore site. As if spewed from the bowels of the ships that had transported them, extensive cargoes—providing a unique window into ancient Mediterranean lifestyles—were discovered throughout the excavation. The relics were so vast, in fact, that within a few months of the initial digging, archaeologists had filled thousands of holding trays and were forced to temporarily stop recovering artifacts for lack of storage space.

The historical significance between the loads of the Pisa ships and ancient maritime trading patterns, not to mention the Roman way of life, was the subject of a recent study by Anna Taylor of the Univeristy of Texas Web Archaeology Project.

"When they were excavated, some of the boats still contained cargoes; others were empty," Taylor said. "Obviously, those found with their loads intact are the most useful for our exploration of Pisa as a site of trade. From these we can learn what products were being exchanged and, sometimes, where they had come from. They cannot be treated as a single entity since trade conditions undoubtedly varied across the 7 centuries represented in the find. Nor can they be used to trace the vicissitudes of Pisa's fortunes as a commercial center, since 16 boats is hardly a large enough sample to reflect changing trade patterns accurately. However, each boat containing cargo can provide an insight into the trade network that existed at its particular time and, as a group, they attest to Pisa's ongoing existence as a trade center."

In her report, Professor Taylor noted that ship B, from the second or first century BC, was loaded with amphorae. On yet another vessel, amphorae were found still stacked in the hold. The seals of many of these were still intact and the contents of "liquid residues" had been studied to reveal wine as well as traces (pits) of cherries, plums, and olives. In yet other amphorae were found traces of scarlet-colored sand, originating from the Bay of Naples. During the Roman Empire this was a common construction material, used in concrete. Professor Taylor's paper continued:

The most recently discovered boats, whose contents have not been published in detail, include animal bones, fishing nets, and small items (cosmetics and an incense burner) from Corsica and Phoenicia. The bones of domestic animals show that beasts such as horses, sheep, and goats were transported between ports by boat and may even have been imported. The presence of lion bones shows the conveyance of an imported animal, possibly for the wild animal hunts staged in the arena. There was trade in domestic animals used for agricultural work and food. Exotic animals were hunted, eaten, and kept as pets.

In addition to such items, some boats (such as B) contained personal effects (a sandal, cups, coins) presumably belonging to the sailors. The boats may have conveyed other goods, which were either removed before the sinking or recovered after it. Alternatively, they may have contained organic products, like grain, which have decomposed without leaving any residue. The boats that are empty (such as ship A) cannot tell us about trade links, although we can make educated guesses about their function from their size and shape. From their dimensions and shallow hulls, the boats appear to be coastal freighters and small harbor crafts.

The presence of the latter might suggest a number of small boats running errands and catering to the larger freighters. If the size and structure of the coastal freighters imply that they were not vessels suited to open ocean travel, then this suggests that exotic imported items were not brought directly to Pisa from their place of origin, such as Carthage. From this we could infer a complex trade network with items being transferred to different ships (and perhaps different owners) along the way.

The main trade items found onboard the ships were amphorae containing foodstuffs. Trade in nonperishable food products and wine, frequently in such amphorae, was common in the Roman world, as shown by the large quantity of such vessels found in shipwrecks. Garum (fish paste), olive oil, olives, dates, figs, and nuts were all traded.

In his book, *The Way They Ate*, Dr. Giugliano confirms this gastronomic tradition of the Romans, explaining that Roman eating habits went through several changes over time, thanks above all to contact made with people from different cultures. All this brought about different ways to satisfy the pleasures of dining. The simple cooking of the ancient Romans, rich in flour products and vegetables and with unsophisticated seasonings, such as vinegar, oil, and wine, had been transformed by the first century AD into a refined cuisine, with precious fowl and snails at rich household banquets.

"Garum was the famous fish sauce used by the ancients to flavor just about everything: vegetables, meat, and even fruit," wrote Giugliano. " '[A salty, aromatic marinade, it was borrowed from the ancient Greeks. The poet Martial wrote that it was a precious gift made with the first blood spilled from a living mackerel.]' The garum trade flourished in the Mediterranean basin. From the production areas in the coastal cities of Campania Felix (Pompeii), Gaul (Antibes) and southern Spain, garum reached affluent households as a distinctive product, sealed in small amphorae upon which tags were attached that revealed the origin and producer."

At the beginning of the third century BC, livestock animals were introduced to the tables of the Roman Republic to supply the ever-growing demand of developing urban life. Pigs were courtyard animals and unrivaled donors of meat dishes. According to Varro, nature donated the pig for feasting. Even Pliny gave honors to the pig: "No animal furnishes more food to gluttony than the pig, given that its meat has about 50 different tastes, while that of others have but one."

It is therefore not surprising that among the domestic animal bones found at the San Rossore site were more than 1,417 samples from pigs. This was the largest bone collection, in fact, among the domestic animal category (48.1 percent), followed by cattle (25.1 percent), and sheep and goats (20.3 percent). Even more interesting is that among the pig bones recovered thus far are 502 scapulas—a triangle-shaped shoulder bone—of which 443 (88.3 percent) come from pigs' right shoulders. This is, according to researchers, "a very unusual occurrence both in regards to distribution and utilization."

While experts have been unable to determine an exact reason for this overwhelming number of right, versus left, shoulder bones, speculation is that prosciutto—ham that comes from the shoulder of pigs—was produced using only the most tender part of the animal. Since domestic pigs frequently lay on their left shoulders, that part of the animal would become tough and dry. As a result, the best prosciutto would come only from the right shoulder, then cured by drying and served in very thin slices—as it is still done today.

"The wine trade along the ancient Mediterranean routes was enormous," Giugliano explained. "It reached its high point between the second century BC and the first century AD, when large cargo ships cut through the Mediterranean heading for markets in the Roman Empire. The great number of shipwrecks along these wine routes confirms this, as do the wine amphorae located throughout the western Mediterranean region, not only on the coastline, but also along the riverbanks that lead inland [such as the Arno in Pisa].

"Roman economic imperialism needed many trade routes to export and import products all the way to Rome. What better way was there than by sea? Most of the provinces, or at least those that counted, were bathed by the sea. And it was already known that all goods could be packed in the holds. Great loads, such as marble obelisks, columns, tubs, sarcophagi, as well as less bulky materials like clothes, foodstuffs, glass, precious stones, or ceramics, could be transported by ships.

"The practical Romans also had their sums right: it cost much more to move a load of grain by land for a few hundred kilometers (wagons could only go about 3 kilometers in an hour) than to send it from one end of the empire to the other by ship. If the ship was, therefore, unlucky enough to get caught in a gale, the loss would be compensated by the arrival of thousands of other ships that traveled the trade routes every year."

Shipwrecks throughout the Mediterranean, including the largest cargo ship of antiquity every found, the *Albenga*, illustrate that the amphora was the container-of-choice for trad-ing voyages. Eleven-thousand wine amphorae were found squeezed into the hold of this vessel, which measured 40 meters long and 10 to 20 meters wide. The thousands of amphorae found within the San Rossore site reconfirm the importance of these containers throughout the Roman peri-od. They also reflect the intense trading, particularly of wine, that took place throughout the Mediterranean.

Roman wine amphorae were traditionally stamped on the rim with trade marks before being fired. In the wreck identi-fied near Marseille, many of the 100 amphorae recovered had the family name Sestius stamped on them, followed by various symbols, among which were an upside-down trident, an anchor, an axe, a star, and a hook. Amphorae bearing the same marks, as well as the name of a rich family in the region, have also been recovered at the site of ancient Casa, today Ansedonia, on the Tyrrhenian coast about 100 kilo-meters north of Rome. The stories behind other shipwrecks, including those of Pisa, are similar: amphorae and more amphorae. Both individually and as a whole, they relate the importance of maritime commerce in the ancient world.

In addition to amphorae containing wines and foodstuffs, the ships of San Rossore also carried everyday items such as glassware. While there is no immediate link to the origin of many of these items, Anna Taylor believes that if their provenance can be identified, they might demonstrate contact between exact regions. Even this, however, would not provide proof of trade of these items along the Italian coast, as they could have been the personal property of crew members, rather than items destined for markets.

"What emerges from the preliminary publications of the site," concludes Taylor, "is a picture of Pisa as either a destination or port of call for traders dealing in items as mundane as food and as exotic as wild animals. The items from regions both near and far suggest Pisa's importance, at least at certain times, as a trade center."

Opposite: Archaeologist drawings offer detailed records of the excavation site in Pisa.

CHAPTER EIGHT

THE
RESTORATION
WORK

Superintendent of Archaeology for the Region of Tuscany/Co.Idra

The historical center of Florence, north of the River Arno, contains some of the world's finest examples of Renaissance art and architecture. Here, in the Galleria dell'Accademia, stands Michelangelo's towering statue of David. In the Uffizi Gallery one finds breathtaking works of Botticelli, such as *Birth of Venus* and *Primavera*, as well as the labors of Raphael, Lippi, and Titian. The church of San Marco is a tribute to Fra Angelico, with frescos that include *Visitation* and *Annunciation*. A short distance south, the city's cathedral, Santa Maria del Fiori, sits boldly in Piazza del Duomo. The dome of this white-and-green marble structure, designed by the architect Filippo Brunelleschi, can be seen on a clear day from as far as 25 kilometers. It is no wonder then that it should stand as a symbol of this grandiose Tuscan capital.

Three blocks from the cathedral, at the corner of Via della Pergola and Via della Colonna, there is another building, rarely seen or patronized by visitors. This is the seat of the Superintendent of Archaeology for the Region of Tuscany, a governmental organization of many divisions and a staff of experts in diversified fields. One of these divisions is the Centro di Restauro (Center of Restoration), established in 1966 and headed by Mario Cygielman.

It was here, among the historical treasures of Florence,

that the investigation trail had led me. The archaeological work at San Rossore had presented researchers with a series of unique problems, particularly in the area of restoration. Cygielman, because of his leadership in this sector, carried the overall responsibility for the methodologies deployed in overcoming these hurdles.

Land excavations traditionally provide archaeologists with a determined set of field characteristics, or obstacles, that must be overcome. In some cases, these include the removal of large rock masses or working at locations—often the case in Egypt or other Middle Eastern sites—where water for washing and cleaning objects and instruments is not readily available. Then there are other situations, as in Pisa, where excavations are conducted below the natural water level and therefore require pumps to be constantly active to keep the area from flooding. This, however, was not the only difficulty archaeologists faced at San Rossore.

The Center of Restoration, I immediately noted, faced a seemingly overwhelming task. Imagine if you will the many artifacts that fill the museums of Florence. There are, to be conservative, thousands of objects. Now expand that beyond this single center, to every city, town, and village within the Italian region of Tuscany—Arezzo, Grosseto, Livorno, Lucca, Pistoia, Prato, Siena, Volterra, the island of Elba, and, of course, Pisa. And these are just the major locations. There are hundreds of tiny hill towns, each with its heritage and treasures left by past generations.

Cygielman's team, with regard to archaeological restoration, covers all of these locations, working on numerous projects simultaneously, as they emerge. One of the center's greatest challenges in recent years, however, has been the recovery and restoration of the ships of Pisa.

"The experience acquired by the center's staff in the field of the conservation of organic materials, and especially damp wood, meant that they were not faced with a completely new problem," pointed out Cygielman; "nonetheless, the very scale of the discovery immediately demanded, and will continue to demand, the adoption of techniques that will have to be constantly verified as the work progresses.

"In recent years, both in Italy and abroad, the retrieval of ancient ships has contributed toward increasing the interest in and concern about the problems associated with the conservation of these finds. However, a method of conservation and restoration that can be considered the only one or the best one, regardless of the particular aspects or individual situation, has not yet emerged."

The primary hurdle faced by researchers was the rapid decay of the ship's wood as it was exposed to the elements following 2,000 years of burial. Also hindering the restoration field efforts was the array of materials, including items of cargo intermingled with each wreck and the depth in which they were found. Working with parallel teams on the ship and the artifacts, however, created a systematic method for both restoration and recovery.

"One of the most immediate priorities was to retrieve the wrecks without damaging their structure, by removing the hulls from the excavation area in order to protect the wood and prevent, as far as possible, its deterioration," wrote Cygielman in an initial report. "Hence it was necessary to encase the hulls in a fiberglass structure, a kind of shell that allows them to be moved more easily, in order to be able to proceed with the various stages of restoration in specially equipped laboratories."

And what, I questioned, would the stages be?

In answer, the director of the Center of Restoration said that, "The first treatment will be the immersion of the hulls in demineralized water, with a fungicide, in specially constructed tanks in order to be able to proceed with the desalination and thorough cleaning of all the wooden structures still covered with layers of mud.

"The wood will next be soaked in substances to consolidate it, either by immersing it in a tank or by constructing an air-tight shell that would, however, permit the passage of these substances. It can then be dried and seasoned. Though the restoration of the ships is the highest priority and by far the most complex problem, it is not the only one. The conservation of the small finds—organic materials, ceramics, metals, stone, glass, and so on—will also be an extremely exacting task."

How long will the restoration of the Roman ships take? When might they be displayed to the public?

"So great and complex an undertaking," Cygielman said, "will inevitably take a long time, and one hopes that, from this point on, the general public will be able to view the various stages of the restoration of this major discovery—in accordance with the requisite security regulations—and that information centers will be set up around a work site organized as an 'open' structure [or museum]."

Many believe, although no confirmation is being given, that such a public viewing center will be established in Pisa's historical Medici dockyards. Here already is a museum dedicated to the ships and the recovered artifacts, most of which underwent rigorous conservation and repair processes in the hands of experts employed by the Center of Restoration. This was particularly true with regard to organic materials, not only of wood, but also rigging, interlaced vegetable fibers, and leather.

From the documentation of the center, I found that research teams adapted recovery methods that were "state-of-conservation" based, if not state-of-the-art.

Objects were removed by slicing the terrain with metal blades. Removal of objects enclosed in sand posed the problem of lack of cohesion of sand particles, which hindered our attempts to remove them without adequate containment. For those objects surrounded by clay, on the other hand, there was no problem of removal, thanks to the plasticity of this sediment. Instead, however, it presented us with later cleaning difficulties.

Once rigging or carved wooden objects had been removed, they were placed in wooden containers, previously covered with a film of polyethylene, which allowed us to conserve them at their accustomed degree of humidity. Consequently, they could be conserved right up to the time of cleaning and restoration, carried out at the Center of Restoration in Florence.

After excavation, and removal from the ground, the leather items were, however, washed immediately, on site, to remove earth from them before immersing them in baths of water with antifungal solutions (Preventol R80 at 1 percent) where they [remained for] further treatment.

Items composed of vegetable fibers, such as baskets, mats, and purses, were more complicated to recover because their surfaces, once exposed to the elements, began to decompose immediately. The fragile condition of these objects called for very delicate cleaning and an application of polyethylene as quickly as possible after discovery. The next step of conservation involved making a fiberglass cast of the artifact.

Once the cast hardened, the object was cut from the ground and removed in a block. The next phase called for this so-called block to be turned upside down, allowing archaeologists to clean away the dirt on the underside of the item. Following this, a fiberglass casing was also applied to this area, creating a protective coat around the recovered object.

"At this point," explained researchers Fabio Fiesoli and Fabrizio Gennai, "while the object was between the two sheets, but not, as yet, fixed together with stainless-steel rivets, one or more tubes were inserted in order to allow water to enter. This is a must if the water content is to be maintained at the same level as when the object was discovered."

A large, round, woven basket found in the sandy strata of

the northern sector of the excavations called for innovation in the removal technique, recalled the archaeologists. This was primarily due to the size of the basket (approximately 45 centimeters [high] by 38 centimeters [wide]), which led researchers to believe it might collapse if not recovered by a strategic method; its components were extremely fragile, with little support from the surrounding terrain. Documented Fiesoli and Gennai:

> In order to recover it, we worked out, and put into use, a special technique of encapsulation, which allowed us to work without risk of damage to it. Leaving a 10-centimeter space to the side of the exhibit, we inserted four wooden panels into the earth around the object. These panels were connected by strings so that they would make up the four vertical sides of a container.
>
> The topside of the basket had already been unearthed and protected with a transparent film. It was recovered in sand, right up to the top of the container, then the sand was packed down and fixed in place with an application of a special preparation adapted for such situations (Primal AC33 in a 5-percent solution).
>
> At this point another wooden panel was used as the lid, and the box was closed. All the panels were then

firmly affixed using wire and screws. In order to cut away the underside, a 6-millimeter-thick metal sheet was used. Once this had been fixed to the box by means of previously bored holes, the box was properly sealed. The structure was put into a sling, lifted out [of the excavation pit] by mechanical means and transported [to a restoration center for additional work]. There, the object was placed in the same position that it had been while in the ground. . . . [Here, the side panels were removed] and the basket was freed from the sand and cleaned, protected with a polyethylene film and a sheet of fiberglass, and then resupported with sand.

The box was then sealed again, turned, and the latter process repeated until every side—as well as the internal part—of the basket had received a protective coating. Only at this point could this ancient, handcrafted artifact be freed from the sand and box, while awaiting future phases of conservation and restoration.

All of this for a single basket made of vegetable fibers. This example perfectly demonstrates the time, the study, and the effort put into the archaeological efforts at San Rossore. While the world has focused primarily on the ancient ships, the dedicated researchers realize that no item is insignificant. There is a story behind each object, to be revealed if only the right investigative trail is followed.

Opposite: Archaeologist's drawing of the sailor and dog skeletons, as found in the San Rossore site

CHAPTER NINE

MYSTERY OF THE ROMAN SAILOR AND HIS DOG

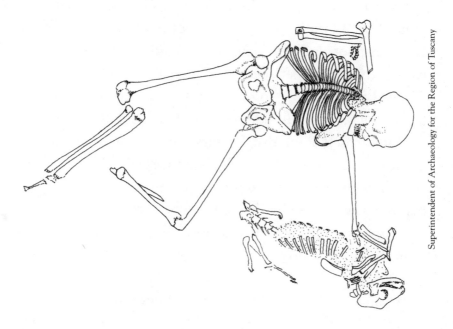

Superintendent of Archaeology for the Region of Tuscany

I n the later months of 1999, as archaeologists painstakingly worked through the excavation site, one of the most dramatic finds of San Rossore came to light near the first-century BC ship labelled B—the so-called honorary ship. It was a fully intact human skeleton that would soon become known as the "Roman sailor."

While this find alone would have been significant to the overall project, there was more. Within an outstretched arm of the sailor was the skeleton of a small dog that appeared to have been a basset hound.

Over the next 4 months, as reporters learned of the find, journalistic fantasies would try to fictionalize the fate of the Roman sailor and the dog. What catastrophic event had caused them to meet such watery deaths? Had the seaman plunged into harsh, stormy waters to save his best friend from drowning and in doing so met his own fate?

Rome-based journalist Richard Owens, writing for *The Sunday Times* of London, speculated that: "A Roman sailor who drowned while struggling to free his foot from a rope as his ship was sinking has been 'brought back to life.' "

I recorded my own speculation on the mysterious man from the sea as follows:

Because no human remains were found, until now, it

was thought that perhaps a tidal wave swept through the harbor at night, overturning and sinking ships that were anchored or pier-side, but killing no one. The new find, however, reveals this to be untrue.

The skeleton of what researchers are calling a sailor was recently uncovered at the site. More interesting was the fact that in the outstretched skeletal hand were the remains of a small dog.

This find, according to Bruni, provides more evidence towards the tidal wave theory. It is believed that when the tidal wave struck, the sailor tried swimming to safety. But, unwilling to release his "best friend," his efforts failed.

In reality, it was later revealed that, periodically, human remains had come to light during the excavation. Most were single bones that analysis indicated belonged to different individuals. In addition, there were three distinct skeletal deposits found in different sectors of the site. To learn more about these, and to obtain greater insight into the identity of the Roman sailor and the circumstances surrounding his death, I turned to Francesco Mallegni, professor of paleontology at Pisa University. Using modern forensic techniques, Mallegni had been tasked to analyze the human remains of

San Rossore and, hopefully, to provide scientific evidence that would help in revealing their stories.

"[The first skeleton is that of the sailor]," Professor Mallegni pointed out. "The second skeleton was retrieved from an amphora and lacks pelvic girdle and lower limbs. It belongs to a newborn baby."

The third discovery was that of a collection of long limb bones—right humerus, radius, ulna, left femur, tibia, and fibula—that appeared to belong to several ancient peoples. In his scientific report, Mallegni wrote: "These bones . . . belonged to about ten individuals altogether. A diagnosis of sex and age at time of death of these deceased (including both the more-or-less complete skeletons and also the single bones) reveals that eight were from males and only one from a female (represented by a single femur). The tenth person was the newborn baby."

In addition to the Roman sailor and his dog, the remains of the baby discovered in an amphora is of great interest. Why in an amphora? And why were its lower limbs and pelvic girdle missing? Professor Mallegni presented this explanation:

Interestingly, the fact emerges that this little skeleton was found inside an amphora and had been decapitated in the manner of the ancients, presumably so that it would fit inside the amphora. The amphora's neck had been sealed originally with a bundle of twiggy vegetation. Later on this vegetation sank part of the way inside the amphora, and this allowed the currents to get inside and wash away the lower limbs of the little skeleton. This is assuming that the corpse was placed in the amphora headfirst and positioned inside it upside down relative to the amphora's neck. So it seems that the amphora was a little coffin prepared for burial, for it is difficult to believe that the waters of the harbor had been intended as the little corpse's final resting place. Perhaps it would be nearer the truth to believe that because of circumstances unknown to us, the amphora accidentally slipped into the waters of the harbor while it was being taken to the necropolis on the other side of the port.

While very practical in concept, I wondered how common the utilization of amphorae as coffins actually had been during the Classical era. Certainly there were unique circumstances, perhaps even the case in Pisa, whereby a family, in a state of depression over the loss of their child, might simply discard the dead fetus in a way that would not draw attention, but Mallegni pointed out that amphorae were frequently used by the Greeks and perhaps even the early Romans as containers for the bodies of the dead.

For more enlightenment on this I turned to Dr. Jon Hall, a senior lecturer at Otago University in Dunedin, New Zealand. Specializing in the Classical period, Hall had spent much of his life studying the cultural and social habits of the Greeks and Romans, including participation in several archaeological expeditions.

"How common was the practice of using amphorae as coffins in ancient times? The best answer perhaps is 'quite common.' It certainly wasn't unusual," said Hall. "Numerous examples are found from the Greek Archaic and Classical periods."

Hall also told me that the custom was known throughout the ancient Greek world, but that he had not attempted any cross-cultural comparisons beyond the Greeks.

In my own studies and search for a motive behind this behavior, I had found a reference to amphorae coffins in Robert Garland's book, *The Greek Way of Death*. In this work, the author remarks: "[I]t is difficult to resist the impression that any serviceable container was acceptable for the body of a child."

I wondered if Hall agreed with this theory. He told me:

I'd agree that practicality was in most cases the driving force. A number of points may be relevant here: at [the archaeological site] Metaponto, child burials were significantly underrepresented in our sample (that is, according to projected infant mortality rates, we would expect to find many more child burials than we did). This underrepresentation is partly explained perhaps by the poor survival over the years of the infant bones (that is, they were there but we simply didn't find them). But it's also likely that many were not buried in the main necropolis in the first place. Some families probably didn't go to the effort of organizing formal burials for very young children (as many as 30 percent of those born may have died within their first year).

This may help to give a context to the use of amphorae, and so on, as a mode of disposal. When child deaths are so frequent, practicality—rather than social display—takes precedence perhaps. (Most young children also, however much loved, probably did not yet have a high social profile to warrant especial social display.)

And amphorae of course would have been ubiquitous in a Greek society that relied so much on olive oil and wine. So they were handy, relatively cheap, easy to fit an infant into, and provided some protection against scavenging animals once buried.

Hall concluded by pointing out that, "The same thing can be said more or less for roof tiles, which were used for both child and adult burials throughout Magna Grecia. A tiny infant can be laid on one inverted roof tile and then covered by a second, the other way up. Larger tombs were constructed for adults from bigger tiles arranged in a more complex way."

Because of the unique position of the Roman sailor and the dog, archaeologists chose to dig them up fully intact, that is to say, removing the entire piece of ground in which they rested so that the skeletons could later be displayed semi-buried, as they had been found. Researchers believe, based on the state of preservation of the man and the dog, as well as the position in which they were found, that large amounts of material covered their bodies after they had fallen into the water. This, according to Mallegni, could account for their anatomical connection.

While several theories have arisen regarding the final moments of the sailor's life, the most feasible, and the one experts are led to believe, is that a sudden rush of flood water in the river caused the ship on which the victims were lodging to wreck, flipping over and dumping its cargo into the harbor. Because ship B, the honorary ship, is the closest to the remains, and was found in a position slopping downward toward the skeletons with part of its cargo beyond its broadside, this is most likely the vessel from which the sailor and the dog fell overboard. Reported Mallegni:

> We have to consider the position of the man's neck, which turns out to have been hooked onto the bottom of a wooden stake that was lying over him, crosswise. This stake was pinned down, in turn, by the rest of the vessel's planking. We have, here, a situation where, in addition to the cargo fallen on top of him, his body was not allowed to float up to the surface. Instead, it slowly decomposed until only the skeleton remained, along with that of the dog, which remained at his side under the planking. Thus we are faced with a situation, which is unique in the history of archaeology. Normally, once the bodies of the drowned have decomposed, the bones drift with the currents and turn up as solitary bones, as was the case with the other eight individuals. . . .

Because all of the human bones found at the San Rossore site thus far, with the exception of the single femur, belonged to men, it is believed that most subjects were dock workers who drowned during various time periods and for different reasons. Once in the laboratory, scientific research and months of analysis seemed to confirm this theory, as Mallegni indicated:

> [O]ur evidence seems to suggest that the men were usually robust, with limbs, particularly upper limbs, showing signs that powerful musculature was once attached to them. This gives weight to the theory that we are dealing with dock workers here, who were accustomed to moving cargoes and rigging around. Moreover, we are dealing with taller men than were ever found in the human groupings of the central and southern Mediterranean, at the time when these remains were alive. They were between 169 and 174 centimeters. Because six of the eight men were over 170 centimeters tall, they may have been (ethnically) of Nordic origin.

Scientists say that the Roman sailor was about 40 years of age and stood 167 centimeters (5 feet 6 inches). While there are several speculations as to his origin, many of the researchers believe he could have been from the region of Naples, where much of the cargo of the honorary ship originated.

Scientific Director Stefano Bruni explained that analysis of residue found in the amphorae of the ship revealed sand from the Naples area. He and other researchers, therefore, suspect that some of the crew, probably speaking a crude Greek dialect, may have been from that area of southern Italy.

During the Roman era, many ships that travelled the coastal waters of Italy utilized slave labor. Most frequently these individuals came from Carthage, Libya, Sardinia, or Thrace. Whether the skeletal remains found alongside ship B are those of a free man or slave is another topic of academic speculation. His physical structure and estimated "old" age, however, would indicate he was a hired deckhand.

"Our Roman sailor was vigorous and strong," said Mallegni, "with the powerful chest of a man used to hard work, such as carrying heavy loads and dealing with sails and riggings."

Mallegni also pointed out the fact that the sailor's upper teeth—in particular, his incisors—had been worn to the roots, most likely from holding ropes. This, they suspect, would also indicate a professional seaman rather than a slave.

And what of the dog? What was his role abroad the cargo-filled ship? According to researchers, it was not infrequent for crews to have canine companions during the long voyages of early Roman ships. Vessels laddened with cargoes such as grain, oil, and wine were particularly susceptible to infestations of rats. Dogs, like the skeletal basset hound, were able to fit into the tiny areas of the ships' holds, and earned their keep by ridding the vessel of such rodents.

Mallegni and his team of paleontologists at the University of Pisa, during 1999 and 2000, did more than merely study the physical and scientific evidence presented by the human remains, including those of the Roman sailor and his dog. Utilizing a technique brought into the twentieth century by Russian paleontologist Mikhail Gerasimov, they took an extensive series of measurements of the sailor's skull, which would lead, ultimately, to the facial reconstruction of the man behind the mystery.

"[In facial reconstruction] the bones of the skull form the frame of the face, just as steel girders form the frame of a building," wrote John Prag, coauthor of *Making Faces: Using Forensic and Archaeological Evidence*, and keeper of archaeology at the Manchester Museum, England. "And just as concrete is poured around the girders to a specific thickness, so the muscles are added to the skull, to thicknesses known from measurements first published in 1896 and updated several times since."

Prag continued, "The technique of facial reconstruction is therefore fully objective: the artist is guided by the rules of anatomy, not by preconceived notions of how a person may have looked."

The actual making of a facial reconstruction begins with a rubber mold and cast, from which a computer-generated resin skull is developed. It is upon this that the face is built. Mallegni's team first took dozens of skull measurements in their analysis of the cranio-facial characteristics. Some of the more important dimensions included those of the eye sockets, width of the jawbone, space between the central eye socket, the upper lip, and the chin. There were also calculations of the width and overall length of the skull.

Once the resin skull is produced, tissue-depth markers, or pegs, are cut to specific depths, based on a universal standard for facial location. These are then glued onto the cast at designated points on the skull. After the markers are in place, they are systematically connected using an oil-based clay. Facial features, such as the eyes, nose, and mouth, are then constructed upon the mapped markers. At this point the skull appears with a clay "skin" matching the natural thickness of the original facial tissue. The artist, having completed this framework, then moves forward to sculpt realistic human features. If evidence suggests hair—including color and texture—this is also added.

In the case of the Roman sailor, Mallegni's reconstruction

of a fortyish man with high cheekbones and strong jaw appears, as reported by the Italian daily newspaper *La Repubblica*, "strangely familiar, as if he had just stepped ashore."

The face, in fact, resembles that of several ancient Roman leaders depicted in statuary throughout the Italian peninsula. In the National Archaeology Museum of Naples, for instance, the marble statue of Marcus Holconius Rufus, from Pompeii, carries a haunting resemblance to the bust of the sailor's reproduction. Given the theories that he may have originated from the Naples area, perhaps even Pompeii, these likenesses may be more than coincidence.

In addition to the sailor and the dog, a considerable number of animal bones were also extracted from the excavation site. During a visit to San Rossore in mid-2000, I was told that 5,111 pieces in this category had come to light to date. While 40.5 percent (2,069 pieces) of these were fragmented and could not be identified, the remaining specimens came primarily from mammals, birds, fish, as well as land and sea reptiles (tortoises/turtles).

Most of the animal bones were those of domestic species (96.8 percent), whereas the remains of wild animals made up only 3.2 percent of the total relics. One of the more interesting discoveries of this latter group was part of a jaw and a tooth from a lion, which came from the so-called Punic ship, because of the cargo it carried (amphorae and pottery from the Punic region).

Researchers Claudio Sorrentino, Zelia Di Giuseppe, and Francesco Manzi pointed out in their report: "Particularly striking was the discovery of a bone that had no place among Italian fauna. This extraordinary find was made amidst a cargo of pottery from a large vessel [in the southern extension of the excavation and consisting primarily of numerous loose timbers, which was], later named the 'Punic Ship,' or 'Ship of the Lion,' in a pile of various types of bones from different animal species. It is the fragment of a left jaw consisting of the front portion still containing a large canine tooth, in an excellent state of preservation, belonging to a lion. Examination of the tooth revealed that the specimen was probably a young lioness. This discovery, given the find spot in an 'African' cargo of amphorae and pottery in the wreck . . . indicates a degree of maritime trade and/or transportation of animals from the African coast to Italy."

Among the domestic species bones represented are those of cattles, dogs, donkeys, goats, horses, pigs, poultry, and sheep. The remains of three horses came from the same vessel, as did the lion specimen. From ship B, the oldest and best preserved of the cargo craft excavated to date, came bone samples from a variety of species, primarily pig (59.6 percent), goat (24.7 percent), and cattle (7.9 percent). There were also two species of wild game—deer (3.4 percent) and rabbit (1.1 percent)—in this ship.

Researchers believe that while some animals went down with the various ships, the greater number of samples proba- bly belong to remains of beasts that were tossed into the har- bor waters or fell in during loading and offloading of cargoes.

Opposite: Designs of various amphorae found in the excavation site, dating from the 3rd to 1st century BC

CHAPTER TEN

MESSAGE FROM A "BOTTLE"

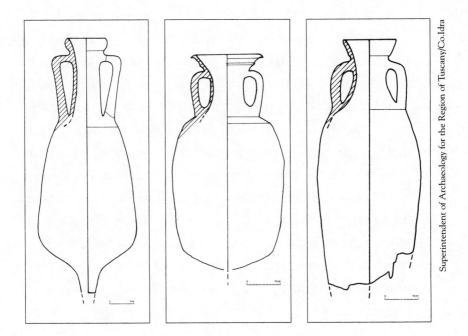

While there is a certain fascination related to finding bones, particularly human, but also animal, the first time I visited the San Rossore site in April of 1999, I was overwhelmed by the array of artifacts from daily life. I had arrived expecting to see ships, and I did. What I was not expecting were the *tons* of amphorae, ceramics, pottery, glassware, coins, fabric, and other items, each telling a story of ancient Mediterranean life.

"Besides the extreme delicacy of the fieldwork required both by the material and by its context, numerous problems arise from the urgent need to ensure the long-term survival of such an exceptionally large and diverse body of artifacts in the most varied of materials," explained Angelo Bottini, Superintendent of Archaeology for the Region of Tuscany. "Some finds are those normally encountered in sites of the Roman period, for example, the thousands of transport amphorae with their varied contents that have already come to light; others, however, are in such organic materials as wood, leather, wicker, and bone. . . . Thus [the necessity for a] full range of expertise, deployed for this project; from excavation to measurement and conservation, each of us is committed to presenting a correct and up-to-date picture."

Digging in small, gridded areas, archaeologists meticulously recorded the position of each item and its location with respect to the overall excavation zone before removing it. These records, often including drawings or photographs, provided researchers with insight that would allow them to speculate, among other things, from which ship each item had come. In many ways artifacts comprised the primary pieces of the archaeological puzzle. Once placed together, in the proper sequence, archaeologists had an image of the harbor floor as it once was, and the treasures that had collected there over the centuries.

Perhaps more important, though, was the laboratory research. In these antiseptic areas located throughout Tuscany, each object recovered was scientifically analyzed. These objects included not only wood samples from the ships, but ceramics, glass, nails, carved bone objects, surgical and pharmaceutical instruments, and even rocks. Everything went through a series of examinations in search of clues to their origins.

Under the direction of the Superintendent of Archaeology, Dr. Gianna Giachi and Dr. Pasquino Pallecchi employed microscopic evaluation of each find. Chemical compositions were then determined by an RX microanalysis in conjunction with electronic microscope scanning. In a subsequent phase, mineralogical characteristics were determined through diffractometer RX.

Utilizing infrared spectrophotometry (FT-IR) and gas chromatography (MS-GC) techniques, residue samples were analyzed, giving researchers insight into the contents of the ancient amphorae, in particular the juices of fruits, nuts, and olive oil.

Ceramic material recovered in vast quantities at the San Rossore dig were also studied. Archaeologists believed that determining the exact material used in construction might enable them to pinpoint their geographical origins. At the same time, stone recoveries underwent petrography analysis to determine the lithology and, through observation of morphology, their various uses.

Instruments of metal, such as coins, nails, and small items found within the ships, were studied to determine the exact composition, while wood samples were analyzed to discover the type of wood and methods of construction. Researchers had hoped that this information would ultimately lead them to the geographical region in which each ship was built.

In their preliminary report, Giachi and Pallecchi, noted that:

The samples analysed [from the amphorae] so far show that some of them were used to transport solids: sands and pigments. . . . We are not dealing with materials that originated locally. On the contrary, they are from a volcanic area, such as Campania or Latium [around modern-day Rome and Naples]. It would be interesting to discover whether the sands were being transported only as ballast, or for other purposes. Their grain size and composition are those of thinners used in the preparation of ceramics.

The pigments recovered so far from inside the amphorae take us back to realgar and red ochre. Realgar is a reddish-colored arsenic sulphide (As_2S_3), which the ancients called *sandaraca* or *sandaracha*. According to Vitruvius, the best-quality sandaraca came from Pontus, near the River Hyspanis, although Pliny believed it came from the Island of Topasos in the Red Sea. Ochre was a pigment in everyday use. It could have originated elsewhere; but some writers claim that the best ochre came from the city of Sinope, in Pontus, from Lemos in Cappadocia, from Egypt, or from the Balearic Islands.

While scientific analysis continued, so did research into the various amphorae types found in Pisa's San Rossore excavation. Working under the direction of Co.Idra, the organization tasked with the central archives and documentation of the project, archaeologists put hundreds of hours into this effort. The results were detailed reports in six distinct areas, including Greco-Italia, Dressel, and African amphorae, as well as their inscriptions and the *dolia* (large ceramic lids) that had once sealed their contents.

"Amphorae were the containers par excellence for sea and river transport," explained Barbara Ferrini, the archaeologist responsible for recovered materials. "They were produced and sold not for their intrinsic value, but to hold other products, especially oil, wine, fruit, fish sauces, salted fish, and many other commodities. Generally, workshops [for amphora production and sale] were built at locations connected with inland agriculture, along the main roads, at sea and river ports. . . ."

Ferrini pointed out that an important, local amphora factory and a major source for the containers originating from this area was the Ager Pisanus. Upon filling an amphora, it would be sealed with terracotta, wood, or cork plugs. The name of the manufacturer of the product within the amphora would frequently be stamped into the neck, handles, and edges. Also found here might be the name of the distributor or seller of the goods, along with details of the contents, the quality, and the weight.

"Those made with a stamp, generally within a rectangular cartouche, were impressed on the amphora before firing,"

Ferrini explained, "while those incised with the *tituli picti*, were added after firing."

At this point, the filled and sealed amphorae would be loaded and stowed into the bowels of the ship in alternating rows and on top of each other. This method of precise loading and stowing—often using tufa bricks, stones, and other objects to block the amphorae in place, then cushioning the spaces in between with, among other readily available items, olive vines—ensured, for the most part, a stable cargo during the voyage.

Ferrini said that, "Upon arrival at their destination, the amphorae were no longer useful as containers, but often they were reused as material for construction. Their characteristics made them excellent for drains and to lighten vaults or domes.

"Their shape is indicative of the location and period of production, and of the contents. Careful study, therefore, can provide a great deal of information about ancient commercial activities and routes."

But what does an archaeological team do when a 2-ton trove of amphorae is dumped in their laps? Where does the work begin? What is the process of organization and documentation?

According to Debora Giorgi of Co.Idra, the next link in the scientific chain, following the initial field work—that is, the actual digging, the preliminary recording, the cleaning and the reassembling of pieces, where possible—is attempting to establish a time-life (date) and classify each piece into a historical content (geographical origin). To achieve this, a hierarchy had been established within Co.Idra.

At the top were the overall project coordinators, such as Giorgi. Below them were managers responsible for the excavation site operations and the research of recovered materials. Supporting each of these two areas were teams of talented and dedicated archaeologists, divided into groups to fulfill the various scientific work required. Because of the quantity and diversity of recovered amphorae, a squad of seven researchers was assigned to this area, consisting of Elisabetta Abela, Barbara Ferrini, Marco Firmati, Stefania Pesavento Mattioli, Stefania Mazzocchin, Marcella Giulia Pavoni, and Elena Rossi.

To ensure that no research was left undocumented, individual team members, or groups of members, were assigned to follow the studies, conduct research, and present reports relating to the amphorae of San Rossore. Among the topics were epigraphy, African amphorae, Dressel-type amphorae, and *dolia*.

Archaeologist Elena Rossi had one of the more interesting, as well as complex, areas of study: the Greco-Italic amphorae that were found in the south extension of the excavation site.

"During the Hellenistic period, widespread use was made in maritime transport of the type of amphorae labelled Greco-Italic, a term that fully reflects the Pan-Mediterranean, Greco-Roman nature of trade in this period," explained Rossi. "While these amphorae retain some of the characteristics of the earliest Greek examples in terms of shape, they also begin to take on an appearance more closely linked to the western Mediterranean through their slender, elongated body."

Fernand Benoit first used the term "Greco-Italic" in 1954, after discovering several examples of this type of amphorae in the wreck of Grand Congloué, near Marseille, and realizing they did not fit the physical characteristics of the more common Dressel-class amphorae (named after Heinrich Dressel, who compiled the first table of amphora forms in 1899, which was later revised by D.P.S. Peacock and D.F. Williams). These wide-bellied, triangular-shaped containers, with relatively short necks and slanting rims, were common throughout the Hellenistic Greek world as well as the Roman Republic. Numerous examples of the Greco-Italic-type amphorae have come to light in recent years around the Mediterranean. This is particularly true in Sicily, where a large deposit of Greco-Italia amphorae was discovered in the excavations at Gela.

From the report filed by Elena Rossi, I learned that: "Evidence of heterogeneous provenance has certainly done little to facilitate the identification of one single area of production for this type of amphora, and most writers on the subject agree that the same form of container was adopted in different countries. The first attempt to classify this type of amphora was made by Lyding Will, who divided the vast range of Greco-Italic variants into five chronologically consecutive subsets (Forms A to E), pinpointing the various centers of production on the basis of morphology, stamps, and archaeological contexts. . . . Criticism of the chronological and typological differences between the Forms A and D proposed by Will and of the difficulty involved in defining the traditional Form B is forcefully expressed by D. Manacorda, who also holds that the term Greco-Italic has by now outlived its usefulness and that the criteria of evolution should be replaced to take into account production associated with many sites in Megna Graecia and Sicily. . . ."

In 1986, Manacorda suggested that Greco-Italic amphorae should be classified in four chronological stages spanning, in general terms, the periods from 425 to 350 BC, 350 to 325 BC, 325 to 250 BC, and 250 BC to 50 AD. At this point in time amphorae evolved into what, today, falls into the first period of the Dressel-type classification.

"The span of time between the diffusion of the earliest and the latest forms [as mentioned by Manacorda] is quite long, and the reconstruction of the historical events of the years between the first and second Punic wars is highly complex," wrote Rossi. "Manacorda indicates the moment after the second Punic War (end of the third century BC) as a turning point, in that specimens were less numerous in the preceding period but are increasingly documented in the first half of the second century BC, thus documenting the political and commercial expansion of Rome in these years."

In recent years some scholars have suggested new, even later classifications of the Greco-Italia amphorae, to span a period from the second half of the fifth century BC to the Roman conquest of Syracuse in 211 BC. For the most part, however, researchers rely on the original system established by Will. It was this method, in fact, that archaeologists applied to the numerous and varied specimens of Greco-Italic amphorae found in the San Rossore excavation site.

In her initial report, published in early 2000, Rossi delved into the complexities of the finds and the research carried out up to that point:

The quantitative data of the finds indicate that this

type of amphora is present only in the southernmost sector of the excavation area, which proves to be the oldest part of the harbor. In particular, while the area of the pier has yielded Greco-Italic amphorae belonging to the earliest type (late fourth to early third century BC), in the area of the Hellenistic or "Lion" ship located further north, the bulk of the cargo consists of more evolved Greco-Italic types, together with late Massalian and Punic amphorae, many of which are intact and still sealed.

The southernmost sector of the excavations has yielded the remains of a pier built of large blocks of stone laid without mortar, which collapsed sometime around 400 BC, and a series of fallen poles that presumably formed a palisade. The items found against the collapsed pier include two amphorae, identifiable as early Greco-Italic and as belonging to the A of the Will's classification. . . .

Both amphorae are similar in shape and texture, and each has lost its pointed bases. When archaeologists removed these items from the excavation site, they assigned one a reference number of 800, and the other 801. At closer analysis, the first revealed a less compressed body and a slightly longer body, measuring 72 centimeters. The second specimen, that numbered 801, is 64 centimeters high. Each has a body measurement—taken immediately below the shoulders of the amphorae—of 35 centimeters.

The report continued:

The fabric is also quite similar, being fine-grained with very small inclusions (orange in the case of number 801, pinkish-brown in number 800). The slip is beige, tending towards grey in both cases. The numerous shells attached to the surface indicate a long period spent under water. The presence of pitch residues indicate that they were used as containers to transport wine, as is abundantly documented for this type of amphora.

The chronology put forward makes it possible to suggest that both amphorae fell into the water in this area of the harbor basin near the bank, probably during unloading and possibly from the same ship from southern Italy, and then settled against the structure of the already collapsed pier. This demonstrates that the area of the harbor in question was still in use in the late fourth to early third century BC.

The sector just to the north of the pier has yielded

various timbers of considerable size and sections of planking, probably belonging to a large ship that was destroyed in a particularly violent shipwreck. The numerous finds include onboard equipment and cargoes. Largely one on top of the other in a mass oriented northeast to southwest, the material includes Punic and Massalian amphorae, together with a large number of fairly advanced Greco-Italic specimens. . . .

The bulk of the Greco-Italic amphorae, which very probably formed part of the cargo of the Lion [or Hellenistic] ship, can be assigned to the advanced type, elegant in shape and unquestionably easier to handle and stack than the earlier type. . . . The body is more slender and balanced, with heights ranging from 75 to 98 centimeters. The rim is less inclined than in the earlier type. The neck is longer. The handles have an oval cross-section and the characteristic sinuous profile.

The maximum width of the body below the shoulder is 32–35 centimeters, and thus remains much the same as for the earlier type. The pointed base is more solid and is harmoniously connected to the gradual tapering of the lower part of the body. While little information can be obtained as regarding the measurement of capacity, this type appears to hold twice its own weight. These amphorae underwent a period of marked expansion in the first half of the second century BC, and many specimens have been found, especially in Sicily and Spain, on the coasts of southern France, in Carthage, and in Greece.

Morphological considerations lead us to suggest that these specimens can be compared with the Greco-Italic amphorae found on the island of Lavezzi in Corsica and in the wreck of the *Chretienne* C at Saint Raphael. While the main centers of production are located on the Tyrrhenian coast between Cosa and Napoli, there is also evidence of production in various parts of southern Italy (Metaponto, Taranto, Naxos, and Kamarina).

The large amount of material discovered in the area of the Pisa-San Rossore railway station is now undergoing petrographic analysis on a vast range of specimens. The findings will certainly furnish abundant data upon which to base a thorough study of materials in order to identify the specific areas of production.

Reading Elena Rossi's report, and those of other members of the scientific team, increased my knowledge and curiosity of ancient amphorae. It was amazing to me that scholars like Will and Dressel could spend entire lifetimes focused on classifying these widely diverse utensils used by ancient Mediterranean civilizations. And yet, Heinrich Dressel, a man trained in biological methods of classification, had done exactly that, from 1845 to 1920. He created a numbering system for ancient amphorae, based on size, shape, and design. Other classification methods—the Beltram system, the Haltern, the Lamboglia, the Will—would be used by archaeologists, but Dressel's remains the most popular, even today.

While there were several reports on the amphorae recovered from the San Rossore site, it was one written by Barbara Ferrini, an archaeologist assigned the study of Dressel-type artifacts, that illustrated how a single object, such as an amphora, could play a significant role in revealing the secrets of an excavation. When put into that context, it became clear to me the true importance of these objects, and therefore one's desire to study them in great detail.

"[Based on current data] . . . an extremely interesting picture emerges concerning the Dressel-type amphorae, of provincial as well as Italic manufacture," explained Ferrini. "Unlike the earlier Dressel types, this model is better suited to transportation and stowing, being lighter and less bulky. Its form was inspired by Greek models, especially those made on the island of Kos, also used for carrying wine, though never in competition with the Dressel types."

The Dressel amphora was the most frequent type found in the Pisa excavation. This, according to Ferrini, is not surprising, as this had become the most widely used container for wine transportation throughout the Mediterranean from the middle of the first century BC through the second century AD.

Characterized by a long, cylindrical neck and rounded rim, these amphorae swelled below the shoulder, which tapered elegantly along the body. One of the identifying aspects is the double handles these containers support, which made them easy to maneuver. The Pisa examples range in height from 94 centimeters to 110 centimeters.

"Concerning the area of production," said Ferrini, "we have evidence that there were workshops in Campania, Latium, the Adriatic area, and in both southern and northern Etruria, [in particular, the ancient production facility found in the Ager Pisanus]. During the Augustan period, but especially in the early to high empire, these central Italian products were beginning to be imitated by provincial workshops, particularly in Gaul and the Iberian Peninsula. Initially both regions produced amphorae similar to the Italian models, but with time they developed their own identifying features and were distinguishable by their fabric, surface treatment, and production techniques."

Greater research also revealed a large number of Dressel-type amphorae suspected to be of Spanish origin. From area 4 of the excavation site, the factory stamp "MV" was found on the neck of one amphora. Researchers, recognizing this as the symbol of a factory along the Tarragonese coast, stretching from modern-day Barcelona to the Ebro River of Spain, were able to confirm their earlier speculation on the origins of some amphorae.

Red-brown in color, these distinctive containers taper more rapidly than their Italic cousins and, in many respects, parallel those found in the wreck of Petit Congloué, in Marseille. These latter were Dressel-type amphorae from 10 to 30 AD geographically produced in regions of northern Spain.

Containers of this type, from San Rossore, "are most in evidence—sometimes in a ratio of 2:1 to their Italian counterparts—in areas 4 and 2 of the excavation," Ferrini pointed out.

This is the area of ship C, the so-called canoe. Researchers believe, however, that the amphorae are more likely connected to nearby ship E, which is still being excavated.

From Ferrini's report, I could easily see how the Dressel-type amphorae had, among other things, "told" researchers of their Greek-inspired design, linked closely to the Island of Kos. They had revealed, in some cases, origins of the Tarragonese region, thereby confirming that the Pisan trade routes were linked to areas of Spain. In addition, they had provided a time frame that archaeologists could relate to the ships from which the containers may have come.

The secrets of San Rossore's amphorae did not stop here, however, nor did my education about them. From the lower-level hold of ship B, the cargo vessel nearest the ancient wharf, came a collection of 20 intact amphorae. These, for the most part, were produced along the Adriatic coast of Italy and, like others found in this area, were used primarily for the transport of wine and *garum*.

Archaeologists Stefania Pesavento Mattioli, Stefania Mazzocchin, and Marcella Giulia Pavoni had been tasked with the study and documentation of these finds. Their research provides not only details on the amphorae of ship B and the products within them, but also insight into the Roman life style and maritime trading.

Of the 20-odd amphorae examined [from wreck B], 12 were produced along the Italian Adriatic coast over a period probably stretching from about 30 BC . . . to the beginning of the first century AD. . . . These amphorae were originally used in the marketing of wine. The other materials (sand, fruit, etc.) found in some specimens would appear to indicate subsequent reuse, which could also account for the presence of amphorae produced in different periods on the same ship.

The products enjoying vast circulation in Roman times include fish preserved through salting (*salsamenta*) and sauces derived from fermented fish. The use of the latter, both in the medical field and for consumption as food . . . The primary product was *garum*, a clear liquid, often mixed with wine, herbs, or spices, and obtained from the prolonged fermentation of a vast variety of fish (including mackerel, sardines, and tuna, but also small crustaceans) in the sun, together with salt and aromatic herbs. The thick, dark residue derived from the production of *garum* was known as *hallec*. [Other products like] *liquamen* and *muria* were probably the result of distinct later stages in the filtering of this mixture of sun-fermented fish and salt.

Present in nearly all the recipes of Apicius, but deprecated by some authors because of both their cost and their smell, these sauces must have been produced practically all around the Mediterranean by techniques still in use today. . . .

While containing a vast collection of amphorae originating from the Adriatic region, ship B also contained specimens from Spain, including Dressel type, used to transport fish preserves and sauces. Research indicated that these were produced in the Baetica province, along the coast of the Strait of Gibraltar. There were also two examples of Baetica amphorae used, according to inscriptions, for trading preserved olives or wines at the end of the first century.

The fact that there were few inscriptions located on the amphorae of ship B provided useful data to archaeologists, as indicated by the report of Mattioli, Mazzocchin, and Pavoni:

Although Adriatic amphorae are normally among those most often stamped, only three of these specimens are. Two Lamboglia-type amphorae bear the same stamp, "C(ai) Iuli Zoeli," a name suggesting descent from a freedman (Zoilus/Zoelus is a Greek name, thus suggesting slave origins). The link between this stamp and two fragmentary specimens from Carthage make more precise interpretation possible.

The stamp "L(uci) Salvi" found on a Dressel amphora is far better known, as it appears on both Lamboglia and Dressel specimens in northern Italy (Aquileia, Padua, Verona, Modena, Ivrea), on no fewer than seven amphorae from Magdalensberg, the commercial emporium Noricum, and an amphora found on the eastern coast of the Adriatic, in southern Italy, and at Fos near Marseille. The stamp is a precious chronological marker. Its presence on both Lamboglia and Dressel specimens demonstrates a continuity of production between the two types but does not extend beyond the end of the first century BC, a date confirmed by the Augustan contexts at Verona and Modena.

[In regard to] . . . the person referred to in the stamp, although the gens Salvia is quite widely distributed, working hypotheses point towards the area of Venosa in Apulia, where this noble family is documented and where a Lucius Salvius Luci filius was *duumvir* during the reign of Augustus, or towards Piceno, where the gens Salvia is documented at Urbisaglia. The archaeometric analysis now under way may help to pinpoint the area of production.

From the period of Augusta also came a type of amphora not to be found in the Dressel classifications. While resembling a Form 10 amphora under Dressel's grouping, the so-called Haltern 70 specimen was discovered is area 2 of the excavation site. Once restored, the fragmented container demonstrated a flared rim, a conical neck with vertical strap handles, and rounded shoulders. The light hazel color runs along the 75-centimeter high exterior.

"Haltern 70 amphorae have been identified as containers produced in Baetica on the basis of their presence on the same commercial circuits as Dressel, types 7–11, with which they are often linked by the wrecks in which they are found, their morphological characteristics, and the composition of the material," explained Mattioli, Mazzocchin, and Pavoni in their report. "They were widespread throughout the Roman West, as is demonstrated by the specimens found along the limes of the Rhine as well as in Brittany, France, wrecks along the coast of Narbonne, Carthage, Rome, Pompeii, Ostia, and of course Spain."

Researchers believe that from the Augustan period through the latter part of the first century AD, the Haltern 70 containers were commonly employed for the shipping of wines from the vineyards of Baetica. The inscriptions, or *tituli picti*, found on Haltern 70 amphorae generally reveal that they carried *defrutum*, a wine derived by heating concentrated juice, commonly known as *must*, that has been pressed from grapes before it ferments. Used primarily for cooking, *defrutum* was also consumed as a low-grade drink. Other uses of this product included mixing it as a preservant in olives or for diluting better-quality wines.

In 193 AD, Lucius Septimius became emperor of Rome. He would reign, under the name Severus, for 18 years, until his death in 211. During this period, maritime trade expanded rapidly throughout northern Africa, as the Africans provided Rome, and the entire eastern Mediterranean, with oil, wheat, and preserved fish, among other goods. Rich in resources, commerce with Africa would consistently grow for the next 500 years. It therefore came as no surprise to archaeologists when the northern part of the San Rossore excavation site, particularly sectors 1, 2, and 5, revealed a selection of African-produced amphorae from the period of the late empire (350–500 AD).

"Because of the particular conditions under which this material . . . was deposited and the forces to which this area was subject, few of these amphorae are well preserved and fewer still can be entirely recomposed," explained Elisabetta Abela, the archaeologist responsible for documentation of the African amphorae. "However, one [specimen] is of special interest. It is a very long, cylindrical amphora with a rounded rim, low conical neck, and the characteristic small, thick strap handles with vertical grooves. Its cylindrical body ends with a solid point with a molded profile and a flat base. This example is one of the 'great Africa' group of amphorae . . . characterized by its capacious, cylindrical body."

Studies revealed that this container was produced in the region of modern-day Tunisia. Manufactured in reddish clay in the first half of the third century AD, the outer surface has become a light yellow with age and use.

In this same area of the excavation was found an amphora, along with its cork top used to seal the products within. Measuring 90 centimeters high and a maximum diameter of 27 centimeters, this specimen stemmed from the fourth to fifth century AD.

Abela pointed out in her official report that, in addition to other specimens, two of the best-preserved amphorae were recovered near ships E and F:

Their surfaces are paler than the [the traditional] pinkish-tan, and they have sharp vertical stripes. They were discovered in pieces and partly reassembled, minus their lower sections, which unfortunately have not survived. Their cork stoppers were, however, still in place. They were of various diameters, and this time we had clear trace of their contents: they had been used in the oil trade.

Other, similar containers come from a cargo found in area 1 to the west of the first ship to be excavated (ship A). Ship A also yielded some small amphorae with hemispherical bodies; together with the cargo, which is still being excavated, were found bricks and rocks used as ballast, along with wooden elements, plants, and timbers from a still unidentified wreck, which would seem to be distinct from ship A.

Other *spatheya* have been recovered in the northern area.... A few of these came from two deep trenches, situated to the north of ship D, but the stratigraphic clone from east to west does not preclude their belonging to the cargo identified in area 1 [of the excavation]....

Others, of which only the points are complete, have been recovered in an alluvial stratum to the south of ship D, around its stern, along with a large quantity of African light *terra sigillata* and African utility ware that is still being excavated. The stratigraphy would seem to exclude the possibility of any direct relationship with ship D, making this deposit subsequent to the wreck.

It should thus belong with another, as yet unidentified, wreck, and it is not unlikely that a glass container of the fifth century AD, and found nearby but at a higher level, belongs to the same group.

While archaeologists worked diligently to reveal the secrets of recovered amphorae specimens, researcher Marco

Firmati dedicated efforts toward the *dolia* that had been found at San Rossore, particularly around wreck E. These round covers with large, semicircular central handles were commonly used in connection with large Dressel amphorae and, because of the inscriptions they frequently supported, can sometimes provide greater insight into a cargo than the containers.

"[Wreck E] itself . . . has still yielded no direct evidence of *dolia* (only a few body fragments from between wrecks B and E); however, the fragments of Dressel amphorae produced in Tarragon and found dispersed over this area could be taken to indicate that this was a ship laden with *dolia*," said Firmati.

"The connection between Dressel amphorae of Tarragonese production and *dolia* is in fact documented by three of the six known wrecks of such ancient 'tankers' (Petit Congloué, Diana Marina, and Ile Rousse). These, along with the contemporary wrecks with Campanian Dressel amphorae and *dolia* (Ladispoli, Grand Ribaud, La Garoupe), document a particular traffic characteristic of a specific period stretching from mid-Augustan through Neronian times. In coastal Latium and Campania, ships were equipped with locally made *dolia* to transport Italian wine to Gaul and Spain and would return toward Rome carrying wine of inferior quality produced in the Tarragonese region as well as northern Spain."

Thus far six lids have emerged from the Pisa dig. The dimensions and the finger-engravings found—including what appears to be an "F" and an "H"—on a few examples, make these *dolia* comparable to those classified as type A from the La Garoupe shipwreck. The same decorative patterns also appear on the lids from the Diana Marina and Ile Rousse vessels.

The finger-engravings, some experts suggest, may have functioned to ward off evil spirits, something entirely appropriate to the uncertain and risky maritime trade for which they were made. In fact, the function of magical protection is explicit in the phalli, which were often impressed next to the trademarks of *dolia*. One cannot exclude, nonetheless, that these finger-engravings could actually be manufacturers' trademarks, with the letters of the alphabet apparently being some sort of identification.

During my investigation into the amphorae excavated at San Rossore, I had studied reports, talked with researchers, and jotted notes in a large, green, spiral binder as I reviewed the day's activities. It was during one of these evening sessions that I wrote: "While the defined timelines, locations of manufacture, and usage of the recovered amphorae and *dolia* have provided archaeologists with a window—enabling them to 'look' into the past—it will probably be the inscrip-

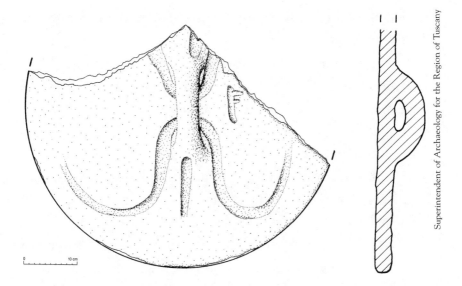

Superintendent of Archaeology for the Region of Tuscany

Fragment of a dolium with finger-carved markings

tions, the epigraphy, of these ancient containers that will be the key with which researchers will be able to 'step' through a door and into the Mediterranean's historical maritime trading. Just as the interpretation of hieroglyphics enlightened scholars of ancient Egypt, so too should epigraphy shed light onto the ships of Pisa."

I had already seen examples of such symbols in various reports, such as that of the Haltern 70 containers and the *dolia.* Given the vast collection of artifacts, however, I concluded that there must be sufficient inscriptions for an in-depth study.

I would soon learn this aspect had not escaped Co.Idra's scientific team. This line of thought, in fact, would lead me once again to archaeologist Stefania Pesavento Mattioli.

Epigraphy is the study, the deciphering, and the classification of ancient inscriptions. Inasmuch as my education of the amphorae types and their contents had revealed a wealth of information, it was this latter area of research that truly intrigued me.

"The inscriptions placed on the amphorae at the time of manufacture and during the various stages in the commercial distribution of the foodstuffs contained [within] are often of great help in establishing chronology and area of production, identifying content, and reconstructing the various economics of a system of exchange that involved the entire Roman world," wrote Mattioli in a report prepared for the Superintendent of Archaeology.

"[Amphorae] . . . generally contain onomastic references, which can be expressed explicitly (*tria nomina*, name of noble family or *cognomen*) or abbreviated using only initials. Persons of citizen-rank are often associated with the slaves, or freedmen working for them, either in the same stamp or in two stamps on the same amphora."

Though much is known about amphora stamps, one question that remains unanswered is why these symbols were so inconsistent over time and geographical region. From the late Republic and early Imperial periods, stamps were regularly used throughout the Adriatic. In other areas, such as the eastern Mediterranean, such markings were completely ignored by amphora manufacturers and merchants using these containers. There is also evidence that within the same workshop some amphorae would be stamped while others would not.

Mattioli explained that:

Equally obscure is the relationship of the stamps to the particular use to which they were to be put, but also to orders placed by the producers of the foodstuffs to be marketed. The extent to which this was the responsibility of managerial slaves, *liberti* and/or the *domini* themselves, that is, the municipal or urban ruling class and even members of the domus Augusta, [is also an unanswered question].

Despite the limitations outlined above, analysis of the stamps has made it possible to identify amphorae produced by the same workshop (though its location may remain uncertain), thus providing considerable

Superintendent of Archaeology for the Region of Tuscany

These drawings by archaeologists at the San Rossore excavation site illustrate some of the stamps found on pottery and other artifacts.

impetus in the reconstruction of the distribution of certain goods, and can contribute to more accurate dating both of the amphorae themselves and of the contexts in which they appear.

In the course of the working life of an amphora, various inscriptions could be painted on it in red or black, often varying in precision and size. These may include dates, expressed in terms of the two consuls, weights, and indications of the goods transported.

The *tituli picti* on amphorae from Baetica prove particularly abundant. In addition to stamps on the handles (sometimes on both handles, at the base of a handle, or on the belly), which refer to the manufacture of the vessel, Dressel oil jars present a variety of *tituli picti* on the neck, with numbers indicating the weight of the empty vessel; on the upper part of the belly, with the names of merchants (*negotiatores, mercatores, diffusores*); slanting along the handle, with the names of the estate producing the oil and their owners; and in the middle of the belly, with numbers indicating the weight of the oil contained. The *tituli picti* on amphorae used to transport fish sauce refer to the type of product contained (*garum, hallec, muria*, liquamen, etc.), sometimes to the type of fish used, to its quality (*flo*, *optimum*, *excellens*, etc.), and to the years of aging before marketing. The name of the merchant or buyer is also frequent.

It is the *tituli picti* that have provided the bulk of information about the foodstuffs transported in amphorae, making it possible, together with Dressel's classifications, to associate specific contents with specific shapes. New information, however, is promised by "labels" identifying contents not conventionally associated with the shape in question. For example, the Campanian wine Massicum specified on Gallic amphorae, wine from Falerno in eastern Dressel [types 2–4] shapes, and probably *garum* in Dressel [type 6A] wine amphorae. These are almost certainly cases where amphorae were reused for goods that had arrived for distribution in different containers. Explicit indication of such reuse was required because customers must have immediately associated various types of amphorae with specific contents.

I couldn't help but wonder—with a smile—if 2,000 or 3,000 years from now, archaeologists finding traces of our own civilization might ponder the strange red-and-white markings that appear on millions of glass and aluminium objects found in excavations throughout the world. Will they, I asked myself, come up with the right conclusion? Will they, after years of study and debate, realize that these were merely the containers of the most popular soft drink of the twentieth century? While it might sound absurd, there is no doubt that a citizen of ancient Rome, in this similar situation, may have considered it ridiculous that scholars would ponder and document so common an object as an amphora. And yet time has proven the contrary.

Opposite: Archaeologists found several shoes, including these clogs carved from wood (specimen 188).

ARTIFACTS OF
DAILY LIFE

In June of 1998 I had the good fortune of working with French archaeologist Franck Goddio in the harbor of Alexandria, Egypt. He was there conducting an underwater expedition that would eventually reveal the sunken island of Antirhodos, where the ancient palace of Cleopatra had once stood. During the weeks I spent with Goddio, I learned a great deal about high-tech archaeological techniques. At the same time, however, daily activities reinforced the importance of grass-roots methodologies. Many of these basic procedures resurfaced as I began investigating the San Rossore excavation.

For the most part, archaeology is a science in which field research is conducted for a specified period of time, often coinciding with seasons or political considerations. During this period, researchers dig, document, and recover objects that are found in a given area of an excavation site. Following the period authorized for fieldwork, the cleaned objects and data collected are studied, and scientific papers are written and published—opening theories and speculations of archaeologists to the academic world to scrutiny.

While this can be an exciting time for some, most archaeologists in my experience—particularly those with an Indiana Jones spirit—dream of those months that allow them to sift through age-old soil, recovering ancient coins, ceramics, glass, and even mysterious-looking objects of unknown use. In this respect, the researchers working at San Rossore were no different. To their delight, there was hardly a day when new discoveries did not surface. Some of the objects were of great scientific value, such as the handful of Roman coins dating from the first century BC to the second century AD.

"Eight coins [thus far have] come from the area where the ships were discovered, and preliminary studies have been made for seven of these; five [additional coins] were found together with other material in the underpass construction site," said Teresa Caruso, author of the study and documentation of recovered monetary objects. "[All of the coins studied thus far] . . . are made of base metal and are of little value. Based on this and the typology of the discovery leads us to believe that the coins could have been lost by chance and would not have been a grievous loss of money, as they were destined for small expenses."

Caruso explained that the denominations represented—*asses* and *quadrantes*—in fact are the smallest of the new imperial coinage. Inherited from the late Republic, these were retained because they were considered the most suitable for everyday expenses due in part to their tiny size.

But what value did such coins have? What, for instance,

could a citizen of Pisa buy with his or her *asses* and *quadrantes?* According to researchers, in the first century AD, one-and-a-half *asses* could put a loaf of bread and a liter of wine on your table. If you decided to wallow in the waters of the public bath, that would cost you one *quadran*, or a quarter of an *as*.

In her report, Caruso pointed out that, "The shopping list, for nine consecutive days for a family of Pompeii, destroyed in August of 79 AD, consisting of food and some occasional necessities, has allowed us to calculate that the daily requirements of one individual, of barely comfortable means, would amount to about 8 *asses*. One should bear in mind that the period between 200 BC and 200 AD was, in the Roman world a relatively stable economical time, with little variation, therefore, in prices and values."

Two of the coins found by archaeologists included one of Gades and one of Granius Marcellus. The first stemmed from the mint near the Strait of Gibraltar and was widely used throughout the Mediterranean region during various periods.

Because only a single example of the Gades coin was found, researchers believe that it belonged to a ship's crewmember. Caruso posed a number of questions—"Did he have it just by chance? Was it a keepsake? Did he keep it to remind himself of home?"—answers to which will never be known.

Caruso's documentation of the Gades coin found in the San Rossore site continued: "The coin of Marcellus also represents a far-flung coinage, that of Bitynia, [which] has been removed from circulation; it is completely and precisely pierced, therefore intended for a specific use, which is not compatible with its primary purpose. . . ."

Struck by an Asian mint, this coin bears the images of Augustus and Livia, side by side. Speculation that it might have been a good luck piece comes not only from the man-made hole at the top, but the fact that, on the opposite side, Livia sits with a cornucopia in each hand. The cornucopia was a symbol of fortune and prosperity in Roman times.

Just as young people tend to do today, the coin could have been worn as a talisman or piece of jewelry around the neck. Ironically, Caruso wrote, "Very probably it belonged to someone to whom it did not bring the good luck hoped for."

There is yet another suggestion coming from archaeologists regarding this coin and that is that it may have been placed under the mast step to bring good fortune to the vessel. It was a common practice during Roman times to position coins such as this to ward off evil spirits and ensure a safe journey.

Wrote Caruso:

The initials "SC" are present on all coins originating from the mint in Rome, and the earliest of these are subsequently to the Augustan monetary reform (20–23 AD). In fact, these initials are typical of, and exclusive to, the denominations, in base metal issued by Augustus after the constitution of the empire, and remained unchanged for centuries. These initials stand for *senatus consulto*, by decree of the senate.

Two coins bear the name of a *tresvir aere argento auro flando feriundo*, that is one of the three—rarely four—members of the board of young magistrates responsible for the fusion and coinage of bronze, silver, and gold [used in producing coins during the Republican period]. . . . Though lesser magistrates with no decision-making power, they have left clear traces on Republican coins. From the end of the second century BC, coins present, in addition to their names, images or scenes regarding their families, their place of origin, their likeness, or current events. In a world with few and slow means of communications, currency became an instrument of political propaganda for the board of three, their *gentes*, and their political affiliations. The coins from the site bearing the names of Lucius Agrippa and Publius Betilienus are the last ones minted by these magistrates, respectively in 7 BC and 4 BC.

The coins found in Pisa—including at least one imitation—carried the imprint of several Roman leaders, including Augustus, Tiberius, Domitian, Hadrian, Claudius, and Vespasian. Caruso pointed out:

Some Roman emperors were deified, and their successors, in part, at least to legitimize their position of power, emitted a "consecration" series recognizable by various characteristics: the individual commemorated shown on the obverse wears a radiant sunlike crown and receives the epithet *divus*. The reverse motifs include the star, the eagle, a circular temple, and various other elements, each symbolizing apotheosis or referring to rites of divinization.

The altar is among one of the most frequent symbols and could represent the alter on which sacrifices to the new god were made or where the ashes were put to rest.

To this second group belongs a *quadrans* of the first year of the reign of Claudius. The most interesting element of this coin is the reverse side in which a hand holds a scale and the initials "PNR," which probably refer to an administrative act, but are not unequivocally interpretable. At least three definitions are possible: *portorium nundiniarum remissum*; *pondus nummis restitutum*; *ponderum norma restituita* (duty at the present time paid; replacement for the total balance; balance you've given up).

Discoveries of medico-pharmaceutical implementations are rare in underwater excavation. Yet some of the more interesting finds among the ships of Pisa were surgical and pharmaceutical instruments. Consisting of bone spoons, a *ligula*, and two bronze *spathomele*, these, experts believe, were part of the "first-aid kits" aboard one or more of the ancient vessels.

"For the moment, those instruments that we have recovered from the Pisa-San Rossore complex are quantitatively few, and are of only two specific types, used in very different fields of medicine and surgery: *spatulae* and spoons, made of an assortment of materials," archaeologist Paola Cillo explained. "These must have been part of the instruments used aboard ship. They were not found all together, but in adjoining areas, and there is good chance that they belonged to ship E, except for one spoon—number 185—from area 4 (ship C). . . ."

While the Greeks were known for their advancements in medicine, the Romans, particularly during the Imperial era, also conducted early medical procedures. As the contact with Greece became more frequent, from the second century BC onward, dramatic changes took place in treatments and the science of medicine in the Mediterranean peninsula. In particular, there was growth in the recording of ailments, the classification of procedures, and the expansion of instruments used for surgery and general medicine.

"Under the category of *specilla*, or probes," said Cillo, "were the instruments used for exploration, dilation, draining superficial boils, and applying medication. Strictly speaking, their use was more pharmaceutical than medical-surgical, in that the little stick could be used for mixing and applying unguents to affected parts. We know from Leonida (Aetius, VI), that they were used . . . to hold down the tongue. A surgical use cannot be excluded for them, however, since Aetius cites their use as the instrument used to obviate vaginal obstruction.

"[Regarding the so-called spoons, or *cochlearia*]," Cillo continued, "their main use was for measuring out the contents of medicines and transferring them to the unguentaries. They are often found side by side with glass unguentaries, which had held medical balsams and unguents."

Other items made of bone and horn recovered from the site include washers, knife handles, whorls, and several hairpins. Twenty-two items of this type have thus far come from the excavation. The area surrounding the Hellenistic ship, for example, revealed two narrow, pencil-like bone instruments. While their exact use is merely speculative, researchers have classified them as whorls or styluses dating, probably, from the second and first centuries BC.

The cargo of ship B included two objects of bone—to which no precise definition or use has been determined—while each of the general excavation areas, 1, 2, 3, 4, and 5, contributed to the items of this classification. A large black, horn needle with three eyes, which experts believe was used to fasten garments "by cleverly passing a thread or small chain through the holes so that the pin closed like a fibula," was taken from area 2. In the vicinity also emerged a knife pommel of the type used from the end of the first century BC through the Imperial age.

Marta Abbado, a member of the Co.Idra team, explained that from the Pisa discoveries, "It is possible to distinguish two major lines in the Roman production of ornaments and small objects: one of prestigious and important works for which ivory is mainly used, the other of minor objects in everyday use for cosmetic purposes, hairstyling, sewing, games, and so on, made of many different materials, including bone, ivory, horn, wood, bronze, noble metals, and glass. . . . Bone is therefore only one of the possible materials, used for this type of object, and is frequently an alternative to ivory; it was definitely more modest, but easy to find and not so valuable. These two materials were probably worked by the same specialized craftsmen, as is demonstrated by the similarities in technique, decorative motifs, and type of artifact. . . . Certainly there was an organized trade in these objects, since many of them appear to have been produced for a local or regional market. The manufacturing shops for the working of bone operated on a complex production circuit, which involved the proximity of slaughter houses [which provided the raw materials] and an accord with other craft workshops, including those of blacksmiths and carpenters."

Of all the objects found in bone and horn, I was most intrigued by the hairpins, which, interestingly, distinctly resemble those used by women today. Long and slender for the most part, and measuring, on average, a maximum of 13 centimeters, these were found in the most recent layers of the San Rossore site. Two large hairpins emerged from area 1, while others, belonging to class AXX, 3 in the Bèal typology, came from zone 2. This latter was probably used to separate hair in elaborate styles as well as hold back locks when makeup was applied. The tentative dates assigned to these items are the third to fifth centuries AD.

Reminiscent of Celtic art is a hairpin from area 4 (number 393) that presents a tiny, decorated top. A more common-style pin used frequently by Roman women emerged from area 5 in three examples.

"During the Roman era, and in other periods, hairpins were much in evidence," said Abbado. "These instruments consisted of three parts: the head, namely a thicker part of various shapes and sizes; the shaft that reached its maximum diameter in the area between the head and the central part; and the point. . . . [These had] . . . three different purposes: to separate the locks of hair during combing and hairstyling; to fix or fasten the hair in different styles; to apply unguents and other cosmetics."

Anyone who has been to northern Africa—Egypt, Tunisia, Morocco, and so on—is no doubt familiar with the region's famed *souks*. In these covered markets one can find an array of locally produced goods, from carpets and jewelry to water pipes and drums. Among the more popular items sought by tourists are oil fragrances. Last summer, in Tunis, the site of ancient Carthage, I purchased several of these, as well as a series of multicolored, glass flasks to hold them.

"These are ancient fragrances," I was told by the shop owner, "used for many of today's famous perfumes. This one, for example," he said, removing the top of a flask and holding it under my nose, "is the Chanel No. 5 fragrance. For centuries visitors have been buying these oil products in Africa and taking them back to their homelands."

As if to validate the words of this Tunisian merchant, 20 balsam oil flasks, of ceramic and glass, have been brought to light from Pisa's San Rossore site. Although only one was found intact, in area 2, the fragments and laborious efforts by archaeologists to piece together these delicate containers, shaped like a spindle or a bulb, provide evidence that they probably date from the fifth century BC through the first century AD.

In ancient times, flasks containing balsamic oils were primarily associated with home use, though they were also in widespread use in funerary functions. They were relatively small in size, much like those still sold today, with an average base width of 3 centimeters and a height of 8 to 16 centimeters.

The ancient Romans, one might conclude based solely on the items archaeologists have brought from the depths of the ancient harbor floor, were very conscious of their physical appearance. In addition to bone hairpins, the northern part of the excavation, area 4, revealed three combs of various sizes, constructed of wood. The soles of three shoes, each demonstrating individuality in the model, were also found. Common features of the shoes included their wood base of approximately 3 centimenters, holes for straps—or laces—and toe latches.

Testimonies of Roman "fashions" were also apparent in leather fragments of a foot strap, located alongside ship C, with an anatomic profile belonging to a sandal. Found as well were aprons and bags, the latter recognized by the stitching holes along the border.

During my excursions through the Tuscan countryside, seeking out scholars and experts in ancient maritime affairs, I came across several contemporary factories producing terracotta pottery and other household items. I stopped at one of these, near the hill town of Castelmuzio, and watched as native clay was worked, fired, and transformed, as it had been done centuries ago, into useful objects.

Ceramics, pottery, and glassware were among the items most abundantly recovered from San Rossore, after amphorae. These objects emerged in an array of shapes and sizes, for varied uses, and from numerous geographical regions.

The southernmost part of the excavation, where stratigraphic investigation brought to light the ancient harbor infrastructure, contained most of the black-glazed pottery, dating from the third and second centuries BC. Included in this group of rich, black houseware were a one-handled cup, a jar, a *kylix*, an *oinochoe*, and several *pyxis*. These, according to researchers, stemmed from workshops located in Volterran and Campania.

Two examples of painted *kalathoi* have been found. The first piece (number 42) consists of fragments from the upper neck and lip, while the second (number 43) was nearly intact with its orangish-brown color and brown-red, painted design. Inasmuch as their appearance differs, both items were classified as Iberian pottery of *sombreros de copa* manufacture. The decorated body of item 43, with horizontal brim and cylindrical structure, makes it easy to understand the "sombrero" name, as it greatly resembles an upsidedown hat.

"The two items found," explained one researcher, "are of different types, and the smaller one appears to have certainly been manufactured in an Ampuritan workshop active in the last 200 years before Christ."

During this same time period—second and first centuries BC—the Mediterranean Sea saw a rise in the use of *lagynoi*, the long, narrow-neck ceramic used for serving wine at banquets, according to Greek literary references. Two of these ceramic objects emerged from the south extension of the San Rossore archaeological site.

The first, number 146, stands 21.7 centimeters high, with

a 3.7 centimeter diameter at the rim and a 7.5 centimeter base diameter. Beautifully reconstructed from fragments, as was the second piece (number 541), the body is a fine gray color, with a slightly rough finish. By contrast, the second piece is hazel-colored.

Lack of decoration on either piece makes it difficult to pinpoint the source of manufacture, particularly since such items were widely disbursed throughout the Mediterranean. Investigators do agree, however, that these pieces fit the traditional *lagynoi* period.

Since the mid-1970s, after scuba diving over the sunken city of Baiae—once the Monte Carlo of the Roman Empire—off the coast of southern Italy, and finding fragments of an oil lamp, I have had a passion for these historical "lanterns." It was therefore a pleasant surprise when I was first shown the beautiful examples that had come from Pisa. Unlike early Hellenistic oil lamps that were simple in form and exterior, those used by the Romans from the first century BC onward were works of art. The spout and body, generally, became larger to accommodate relief art. Simultaneously, craftsmen began to add initials, seals, or names to each piece to distinguish their products.

"The excavation at the Pisa-San Rossore railway station has revealed various types of lamps," wrote Federica Mennuti in the scientific report dedicated to these objects, "such as the black-glazed lamps, inspired by Greek models; the *Vogel-kopflampen*, with their spouts decorated with two opposed birds' heads in relief; the *volute* lamps, with decorative motifs largely of Augustan origin; the typically Imperial disc lamps, the ear lamps, with their side handles, and the *Firmalampen* type, with its channel. Thus we are faced with a vast assort-ment of oil lamps from various ages, some elaborate in their refinement and others fairly basic."

Inasmuch as some of the lamps were certainly destined for commercial sale, most—based on the burn residue found —were probably owned by crewmembers of the various ships. Two lamps in particular—those with black glaze — were found among the remains of the Hellenistic ship, while others came from ship B (zone 3) and from areas 2 and 4. Only one lamp—the *Firmalampen* specimen—has come from area 1.

Produced in various colored clay, the ancient oil lamps, some with handles, others with merely a flat, round base were, to me, a showcase of Roman art. Representations of wild and domestic animals, gladiator battles, chariot races, and mythological characters were depicted. One example, number 249 from the first century AD, has a decorative relief in which a couple are engaged in a sexual act, reminiscent of

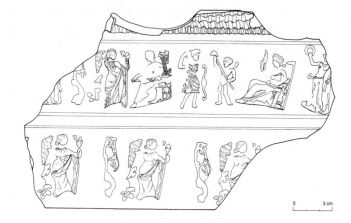

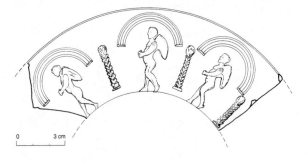

This page and oppoosite: Samples of artwork found on pottery recovered from the Pisa site

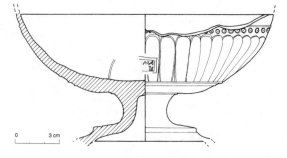

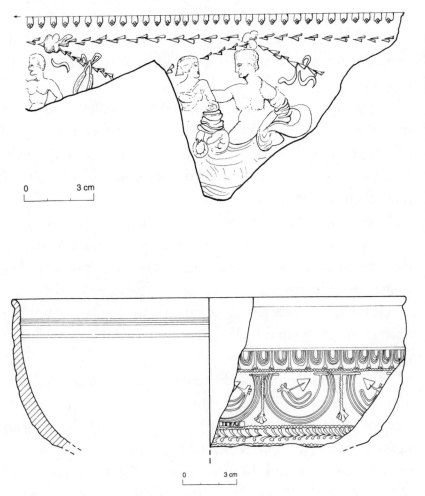

0   3 cm

0   3 cm

the depictions found in the House of the Vetti, in Pompeii. Another, specimen 449, maintains the inscription "L'MVNSVC" impressed on the bottom. Archaeologists attribute this to the trademark of a North African lamp manufacturer.

Just as impressive were the Italic *terra sigillata* extracted from the depths of Pisa's ancient harbor. Produced at the end of the first century, these ceramic items—vases, bowls, plates—boast elegantly molded decorations and a variety of manufacturers' stamps.

Researcher Maurizio Paoletti said that, "Italic, late-Italic and south Gallic *terra sigillata* ceramics are to be found in San Rossore in large quantities. . . . Some vases probably belonged to the cargoes of the ships [particularly B]. . . . Most, however, were simply dumped onto the bottom of the port and/or deposited by the river as its sediments gradually filled the basin."

Why, I wondered, would these beautifully decorated ceramics have been "dumped" into the city harbor? Experts were quick to explain, however, that a major Mediterranean *sigillata* industry, Cn.Ateius, had developed here. It was served by several workshops, some in the northern provinces of Pisa, along the Auser River, and others to the north in the Ager Pisanus. During transit, many of the items were damaged or developed imperfections in manufacturing. These could not be sold to markets throughout Mare Nostrum and were, therefore, trashed in the sea.

Among the decoration of these items is a double procession of chariots led by pairs of centaurs with their hands tied behind their backs (example 217) and the depiction of the triumph of Hercules and Omphale.

"Particularly, we have to mention the presence of graffiti on the bottom of the vases," said Paoletti. "These are for the most part owners' marks, carelessly and often crudely rendered. Other signs, recognized with certainty as Latin characters, are probably onomastic initials, almost always placed on the bottom. This category of inscriptions, varied, but most simplified, could indicate the low level of literacy among the unknown sculptors, no doubt sailors, artisans, or workers at the port of call. . . ."

My reporting would not be complete without mentioning two other categories of finds: ancient glass and *thymiateria*, the latter a term applied to molded terracotta incense burners, sculpted into human figures representing women or deities, of which four have been found—three intact and one in fragments.

Angelo Bottini, Superintendent of Archaeology for the Region of Tuscany, explained that the design of these objects include ". . . small female busts topped with the requisite receptacle [for incense burning], the loss of which has left marks clearly indicating its point of attachment. Whereas the front was molded, the back was only crudely shaped with a spatula. . . ."

Found in the south extension of the excavation area, among heaps of Greco-Italic and Punic amphorae, the incense burners, according to Bottini, ". . . reflect Hellenistic models. More precisely, these items take after a series of late classical, and primarily Sicilian Greek busts."

Throughout their labors, archaeologists recovered various glass items, of which only 20 percent can currently be assigned to identifiable forms. This is due, in part, to the fact that many of the finds are fragmentary. A few glass ornaments—a necklace, a needle—were found in the sandy levels of the northern part of the harbor, but, for the most part, the main items were goblets, beakers, plates, balsam jars, cups, a blue jug with a theatrical mask incorporated into the handle, and various containers with unknown uses.

In a report on the glass items of San Rossore, researcher Daniela Stiaffini wrote, "The items date from the first century BC to the late fifth and early sixth centuries AD. The earliest artifact is a goblet (number 153) produced in a mold, which was found in the cargo of vessel B. In view of its position and its technical and morphological characteristics, this goblet may be regarded as having been manufactured during the first century BC. The most recent artifact is a disk-shaped goblet foot (number 121) discovered in area 5. The quality and morphological characteristics of the glass suggests that the goblet is among those manufactured in the region of Italy from the late fifth and early sixth centuries AD onwards.

"Most of the objects," she continued, "were found in the northern sector of the excavation site (areas 1, 2, 3), where wrecks B, E, and F were discovered. While this part of the site has yielded a notable concentration of glass objects, relatively few have been recovered from areas 4 and 5, where wrecks C and D were found."

Item 202 is of special interest. This hand-blown glass jug, found in area 2, is of blue-green transparent glass with opaque, light-blue filaments. Although it is missing part of its neck and mouth, the cylindrical body of this first-century object is beautiful in shape and design. What really sets it apart from other glassware, though, is the appliqué of opaque, light-blue glass on the handle depicting a female head in relief.

When I questioned archaeologists in the research laboratories of Florence about the significance of the facial depiction on this piece, I was told that it most likely represented a theatrical mask—a replica of one of the many masks worn during open theater performances during the Roman period.

And where would this as well as the other artifacts go from here?

"They will be placed within the Medici dockyards, the structure that houses The Ancient Ships of San Rossore Museum," Bottini said. "The antique buildings will preserve and display these finds, and eventually the recovered and restored vessels, for visitors to view for years to come. Just like the excavations, the museum is a work-in-progress."

And so, my research had made a complete circle, taking me back to where it had begun, Pisa.

Opposite: An ancient Roman coin

THE MUSEUM

In contrast to my first visit to the Pisa excavations, the sun was bright and warm. I stood on the left bank of the River Arno gazing across the traffic-filled Lungarno Simonelli toward a series of old, brick buildings, linked side by side with red, tiled roofs that peaked up and down like tiny hilltops. These were the Arsenali Mediciei, the Medici dockyards, constructed by Cosimo I and his sons, Francesco and Ferdinando, throughout the sixteenth century. A white banner hung in front of the first structure, to my left. On it was printed: "Le Navi Antiche di San Rossore" (The Ancient Ships of San Rossore). This was the final resting place for the artifacts and the vessels that had, after 2 millennia, returned to the light of day. In these historical edifices, the city of Pisa had dedicated a museum to its lost ships.

"It has been decided that the work of full-fledged restoration, in particular of the various ships and boats, will take place in the natural setting of Pisa's Arsenali Mediciei or Medici dockyards," Mayor Paolo Fontanelli had informed me. "This is a structure historically associated with the naval activities of the city and of Tuscany as a whole.

"It is important to remember that the San Rossore excavation, and therefore the museum, are works-in-progress. Additions to the collection will continue as long as the research goes on—which could be for decades."

Viale then explained that the exhibit already contains objects that have been excavated, catalogued, and studied. As the work at San Rossore continues, new objects and ships extracted from the site will be transferred to the spaces, ultimately making this one of the finest maritime museums in the world.

The young councillor explained that, "Set against a background that includes the Leaning Tower and other noted tourist attractions, the lost ships of Pisa will add to the draw of visitors from around the world. Scholars as well as those sharing a passion for maritime history and the lure of archaeology will fall upon Pisa to explore and learn more about these ancient vessels, their origins, and their cargoes. It is certainly a unique opportunity and one that, fortunately, has fallen into our laps."

Following the meeting, as we walked toward the Medici dockyards, Giorgi pointed out that the museum buildings had a length of 59 meters, with width-spans ranging from 9.2 to 10.65 meters and an average height of more than 8 meters. The Medici crest is set on a gable in the middle of the façade and was apparently designed by Buontalenti, who assisted in much of the construction. The crest bears the date 1588, marking the year of completion.

"The rapid decline of the dockyards was," she explained,

"the result of the maritime policy launched by Cosimo di Medici, which assigned Pisa a predominant role as a center of trade and production, but also gave ample space to a series of initiatives designed to develop the western territories of the principality as a whole. Ships were in fact being built at Portoferraio and Livorno even before the Pisa dockyards were completed."

Stepping through the heavy, wooden doors into The Ancient Ships of San Rossore Museum, I suddenly stopped in awe. I had expected a small, dark, unorganized collection of items, perhaps laid out on tables or in boxes. What I saw, however, was a vast, well-illuminated space filled with glass display cases, exhibit panels, maps, photographs, charts, video reproductions, and models. Artifacts that I had seen in the laboratories of Florence, or semiburied in the mud of the excavation site, were now here, clean and reconstructed, complete with description cards and brief explanations regarding their usage in ancient times. Glassware; pottery; oil lamps; incense burners; amphorae of Greco-Italic, African, and other origins; coins; ship's tackle and anchors—all here. In this open display, I suddenly found myself reliving the relics and research of the past 2 years.

There were geomorphological studies of the Pisan lowlands and the city's historical waterways, reproductions of the ancient harbor, and scaled replicas of Roman ships that had been found. In the center of the room was a display of the famed sailor and his dog, including Professor Mallegni's reconstruction of the crewmember's face. Museum management had chosen to display the skeleton in the same manner in which archaeologists had discovered it: lying back-down in the mud, left arm outstretched, skull turned in the same direction, as if to see the tiny dog that lay next to it.

In the distance there was a display of animal bones. I could not help but laugh as I passed one of the glass cases in this section. It displayed two stacks of triangle-shaped shoulder bones—obviously from pigs—that had been found. On the left were the remains of 443 right shoulders, on the right, the 59 left shoulder bones.

Continuing further, I turned and there it was, the pin, the gold fibula that, in the latter half of the third century, had been used to hold a garment in place.

I had truly come full circle. My 2-year-long adventure to put together the pieces of Pisa's ancient puzzle had, in many respects, been successful. There remained open spaces, however, like gaps in an archaeological grid waiting for the discoveries that would provide the information necessary to fill them.

While my journalistic curiosity had been satisfied for the

time being, I also realized that only one vessel, at this point, had been fully extracted. Several others were being excavated and still others remained buried deep within the soil of Pisa's ancient harbor.

The words of Mayor Fontanelli came back to me: "It is important to remember that the San Rossore excavation, and therefore the museum, are works-in-progress."

What will the future bring? What secrets will be revealed as the ships of San Rossore, one by one, are extracted? What will they and their cargoes tell archaeologists? What mysteries will they resolve?

I could only wonder.

ABOUT THE AUTHOR

A former director-at-large for the American Society of Journalists and Authors and Mediterranean Editor of *Scientific American Discovering Archaeology*, Michael Sedge has authored and/or contributed over 20 books, including *Cleopatra: In Search of a Legend*, *The Mediterranean Diet: Origins and Myths*, *Marketing Strategies for Writers*, *The Adventure Guide to Italy*, and *Commercialization of the Oceans*.

During his 25-year journalistic career, Sedge has contributed to most major media, including The Discovery Channel, *Newsweek*, Robb Report, and Time-Life Books.

Founder and CEO of The Sedge Group, a Media/PR/Marketing agency with offices in the United States and

Europe, Mr. Sedge has been called a "marketing wizard" by *Entrepreneur Magazine*. Among his many clients are Arrowhead Space & Telecommunications, AT&T, MCIWorldcom, Holiday Inn, ILOG, and Mobil Oil. More information on Sedge's professional career is available at www.thesedgegroup. com.